100
SUCCESS LESSONS FROM
Warren Buffett

N. CHOKKAN

PRABHAT
PRAKASHAN

Published by
PRABHAT PRAKASHAN PVT. LTD.
4/19 Asaf Ali Road,
New Delhi-110 002 (INDIA)
e-mail: prabhatbooks@gmail.com

ISBN 978-93-5521-489-8
100 SUCCESS LESSONS FROM WARREN BUFFETT
by N. Chokkan

Edition
2026

Price
₹ 400 (Rupees Four Hundred only)

Printed at
R-Tech Offset Printers, Delhi

Author's Note

Warren Edward Buffett is a renowned American business magnate, investor and philanthropist. He is the chairman and CEO of Berkshire Hathaway. Also, known as the "Oracle of Omaha", Buffett is one of the most successful investors in the world. He was born on 31st August 1930, in Omaha, Nebraska. Born to congressman Howard Buffett, Warren had a keen interest in business and investing from a young age. He was only 11 years old when he first started investing in the stock market. While at the age of 14, he made his first real estate investment.

Being business-minded, Buffett spend almost all of his childhood in various entrepreneurial ventures. From selling chewing gums, Coca-Cola, newspapers and magazines to working in his grandfather's grocery store, there was maybe any venture that Buffett hadn't used to earn money in his early days. His father was responsible for the young Buffet's interest in investing and the stock market because when he was just 10 years old, his father took him to visit the New York Stock Exchange.

After completing his studies, Warren Buffett went to work with his mentor and professor Benjamin Graham at Graham-Newman Corporation. There he worked as a securities analyst. Later, he worked as a general partner at the Buffett Partnership,

Ltd. Eventually, he became the chairman and CEO of Berkshire Hathaway Inc., which is an American multinational conglomerate holding company headquartered in Omaha, Nebraska.

From such an exceptional and successful person, one could learn many lessons that could help one become successful in their concerned field. In this book, 100 Success lessons from Warren Buffett, we are going to learn and understand lessons that helped Buffett become successful both in his professional and personal life.

In this book, you will learn about how to do business, how to deal with customers, how to have a work-life balance, how confidence in oneself could change everything, how to deal with bad decisions, standards of living, the value of hard work, the power of habits and so much more.

I hope this book serves as a guide to its readers so that they could bring about positive changes in their lives. It would be my immense pleasure if this could have an optimistic influence on the lives of its readers.

– N.Chokkan

Contents

1

Innovators, Imitators and Idiots

We see innovation in the market all the time. Many companies (and individuals) claim that to be their lifeline. Hence, new thoughts, products and services are regularly being introduced.

However, when we look beyond the quantity (number of innovations) and focus on the quality of those innovations or their long-term results, only a few of them turn out to be transformational and sustained. Others create an initial impression, but later they slowly fade from the market and people's minds.

Warren Buffett explains this phenomenon with 3 I's: Innovators, Imitators and Idiots:

- As the name suggests, innovators are the ones who spot an opportunity that didn't exist before. They look at the existing products and services, constantly think about making them better, ask the all-important 'why not?' question and imagine something new.

- Once these innovators find something new, try it and see some success, these imitators jump in. This is why a fantastic, original best seller book on a certain niche topic is always followed by a series of cheap imitations with similar-sounding titles and wrappers. These people just imitate what the innovators are doing and see some success. After all, it is already a proven idea!
- Finally, we see idiots in the market. These people are worse than imitators because they are here only for the benefits. Their greed spoils the original intention behind the innovation and the whole premise on which it was created.

In our field of expertise, which tag fits us? Are we the innovators who find unique things which solve a real problem or imitators who are happy to go behind a recent success or trend or idiots who only see 'what's in it for me?' in others' creations? It is obvious that innovators are the ones who are going to have maximum satisfaction and fulfilment and the thrill of finding something totally new is priceless!

☑ **The Warren Lesson:** ***Be an innovator.***

2

Tools and their Value

When Warren Buffett talks about modern gadgets and technologies such as mobile phones, computers and the internet, he makes jokes about his lack of understanding about these things and creates an impression that he is too old for these and would never use them right. We also tend to believe this impression because he belongs to a different generation and hence we assume that using modern tools would be difficult for him.

However, a careful look at how he uses some of these new gadgets and tools gives us a totally different picture. Suddenly, he doesn't look like an anti-technology old man, he doesn't look like someone who hates modern creations, instead, he looks like someone who attaches a premium to his time and would only use these tools in the right way. He refuses to jump to a modern tool just because it is new and everyone else seems to be using it. Instead, he looks at it, analyzes it, understands how it can fit in his way of thinking and working and then he decides to adapt it the way he wants.

For example, Warren uses his computer for researching, reading and playing bridge online. He feels these are the main purposes of this gadget for him. Others around him might use computers for trading online or for sending emails. But, Warren has a different set of needs and adapts his computer usage to suit them.

On the flip side, Warren once stated that he doesn't consume podcasts. This is not because he doesn't like that technology, but because he can read faster than he listens.

If you want to know about a certain topic and there are two information sources, an article and a podcast, you don't have to pick the latter one just because it is a modern tool. If you read faster than you listen, picking the old-styled article and reading it is a good use of your time. Instead, if you read slow or if you are driving and can't read, a podcast may be appropriate.

Thousands of people around Warren, even those in his age group, may be consuming podcasts. But, Warren doesn't go by such trends, he looks at podcasts (and other technical tools) from the value perspective and makes the right choice, even if it is old-styled!

☑ **The Warren Lesson:** ***Customize gadgets and tools according to your needs, not the other way around.***

3

Read and Analyze the Raw Data

Let us say for example, you want to learn a topic. How do you go about doing it?

Of course, we research, we read, we understand, we form an opinion and this is the best way to learn. But the question is deeper than that: what exactly do you read? Do you read the source material or the raw data which helps you understand that topic or do you read someone else's analysis, findings and thoughts about it?

When you search for any topic online, you get both kinds of results. It is very easy to read the second category of articles or watch a Video where someone talks about the topic and learn it. Compared to this, articles and sources in the first category are hard to read, digest and make sense. However, when done right, these are the sources that will give you the real knowledge or the exact knowledge you are looking for.

When Warren Buffett researches about a company, he does it the long (and hard) way: he reads their annual reports, understands their business; current state, strengths, weaknesses and future outlook; he then reads about their competitors in the industry to get a complete picture. This is how he understands companies and makes his investment decisions.

According to Warren, we need not read others' reports to understand about a company. Others won't do it for us. We need to absorb information, decide what is important, what is not, relate various items we read about and see patterns. Others can't do this because their views, needs and perspectives about the same data might be entirely different. Our unique information needs can only be satisfied by our unique research.

We can extend this to any topic we want to know about: don't be lazy; read a lot of first-hand information, decide on the important points and use them for better understanding. Others' reports (and speeches) might be easy to consume, but they may not satisfy our requirements most of the time.

☑ **The Warren Lesson:** ***Read the raw data; decide what is important to you; analyse and understand.***

4

Dealing with Gaps

Today, when Warren Buffett speaks, the world listens. If he gives a piece of advice or asks people to invest in a certain company, everyone does it immediately. His word has such a superpower.

But, this was not always the case with Warren. In his early days, he was talking to a lot of people and told them to do certain things. Those instructions were not random, they were based on his research and analysis and he trusted them. Unfortunately, others didn't. They listened to him, but they were not convinced that they should follow what he says.

In this situation, instead of blaming others for their lack of insight or understanding, Warren looked inwards. He started asking, 'What do I need to make sure these people listen to me?'

Note that, Warren's analysis focuses on the gaps on his side, not those on the other side. It is very easy to point fingers at others (or external factors) for our failure and sometimes we may be right too. But, most of the time those things are not in our control. Hence, analysing our own weaknesses (or room for improvement) helps, as we can get actionable insights from those questions.

Back to Warren. His early day self-analysis told him that he lacks sales skills. He took a step back and analysed why he lacks sales skills. He found that he lacks public speaking skills. He decided to act on it and enrolled in a course.

Joining a course is just the first step. Warren dutifully followed the course, applied those principles, got better at public speaking, which in turn improved his sales skills. All these were possible only because he was not afraid of asking that first question and pointing a finger at himself.

☑ **The Warren Lesson:** ***Understand your own gaps and work towards filling them; become a better person every day.***

5

Are you the Smartest Person in Every Room?

If you are the smartest person in a room, in any room for that matter, how cool is that!

Of course, being the smartest person in a group is a fantastic feeling and you get a lot of respect for that. Your views are respected and you may even get a chance to lead the crowd in the right direction.

However, if this continues in every place you walk in, it can only mean one of these two things: you are the smartest person on earth or you carefully decide to hang around people who are not smarter than you.

Warren Buffett advises us to surround ourselves with people who are better than us, because, "you are going to move in the direction of people whom you associate yourself with."

For example, if you are a computer programmer and want to get better at this art (or science), you should start hanging out with better programmers than yourself, you should read their code, you should understand why they have done certain things in a certain way, you should have conversations with them about coding, you should ask them to review your code and share feedback... This applies to every field. People better than us provide us with an opportunity to learn and improve. If this becomes a regular habit, the world becomes a continuous learning platform and we constantly improve from where we were earlier.

On the flip side, if you decide to surround yourself with people who are inferior to you, there is hardly any learning you can get from your interactions with them. Of course, it will feed your ego and make you feel important, but you never know what you are missing.

Hence, there is value in seeking the friendship of people who are better than us in any aspect: they may be quicker in thinking, they may be better in analysing, they may be well-read, they may come with a multicultural experience, they may be more empathetic, they may be good with words, and communication, they may ask better questions... Whatever be the reason, if they are better than us, we can learn from them and constantly improve!

☑ **The Warren Lesson:** ***Surround yourself with people who are better than you.***

6

A Great Deal, Rejected

When people say they don't like the environment they are in, who is the reason for their problem?

Some of the life decisions are forced on us. This means, we don't have a say in them or we don't have enough control to change them. Hence, we need to accept them and move on even if we don't like them. But, many other decisions are made by us. For example, we decide to work with a person or a company, we decide to do business with a store, we decide to accept (or reject) a certain position, we decide to get married, we decide to move to a new city and so on. If these decisions result in a bad environment, we should understand that we are the primary reason for the mess we are in.

But, what do we do with this information?

Next time when we are making a new decision, in addition to considering the data points on the table, we should also think about our previous decisions, their results and map them to the current decision, visualising the possible future. We can't be 100% right, but we can see glimpses of the future and if we don't like what we see, we should either reconsider that decision or do something to ensure that the future is different from what we see now.

Warren Buffett says, he has denied good business deals because, he has to work with people he doesn't like. In other words, he sees a future where he may be working with people he doesn't like and makes a decision in the present so that he needn't be in that situation ever.

Notice the term "good business deals" in Warren's statement. This means those are good decisions when seen from the business perspective. But, when seen from the people perspective (who you will be working with and what energy they bring to the table), they become bad decisions and Warren doesn't hesitate to say no to such deals because for him working with the right people is important.

What if money is more important to you and you don't mind working with people whom you don't like?

In that case, your viewpoint of "important things" is different and you will be making a different decision unlike Warren. That's perfectly fine. There are no rights or wrongs here, as long as our decisions are in line with what we consider as important.

This means, every decision has to be analysed from multiple perspectives and we need to look at the possible future from many lenses (things that we consider important). If we believe something is important and not negotiable, it should reflect in the decisions we make now.

☑ **The Warren Lesson:** ***While making decisions, always consider what is important to you.***

7

Knowable and Urgent

Deciding, whether to invest in a certain company or not, is a tough decision. You need to consider multiple factors, measure them, analyse them, form an opinion and decide based on that. However, while analysing those factors, Warren Buffett says that he only looks at things that are "knowable and important".

For example, the industry in which a company operates, its business, products, services, management team, partners, competitors, possibilities of international expansion etc., are important factors and you can know them with a bit of research. Hence, they come under the "knowable and important" category. We should strive to know these details as much as possible and make our investment decisions based on them.

On the other hand, possible interest rate changes during an investment period may be an important factor for an investment decision, but it is not knowable as no one can accurately predict the direction in which interest rates will move and by what percentage. We can make an intelligent guess, nothing beyond.

Hence, Warren advises us to worry only about knowable and important factors and use them for decision making. This way, we will still be following a scientific approach and not enter any guessing game.

Warren's approach can be extended beyond the investment world too. For example, when selecting which college degree to pursue, a student may consider knowable and important factors such as curriculum, university details, credentials of teaching staff, lab facilities, availability of practice opportunities, higher study options, campus interviews, etc. Focusing on these is better than worrying about important but not knowable factors such as the job market when he or she graduates. Of course, students can keep a watch on such factors and course correct if required, but worrying too much about not knowable factors won't get them anywhere.

Hence, when you have to make a decision based on certain factors, try classifying them as important or not and knowable or not. Suddenly, you will see additional clarity that will help you in decision making.

☑ **The Warren Lesson:** ***Focus on the Knowable and Important Things.***

8

Is Time a Friend or an Enemy?

One of the common aspects you find in the websites of great companies is a section called "Timeline". It provides the history of that company from its early founding days till today, with a specific focus on milestone years and events. They could've provided it as a series of paragraphs, but this timeline view provides a unique perspective and understanding about why this company is where it is today and what made it great.

According to Warren Buffett, time is the friend of good businesses and the enemy of bad businesses. This means, if you have good fundamentals, systems, team, product or service over time, you are likely to succeed. Time will help you make the best use of those strong basics and achieve great things. On the flip side, if your basics are weak, time will only expose them further and make your mediocrity public.

We can see this in every field: when a new idea clicks, hundreds of businesses emerge trying to cash in. But, not all of them survive and taste success. Over time, only a few companies emerge as leaders and others slowly fade away. That's the effect of time. It clearly shows who is strong and who is not.

This is true for individuals as well. When we have a strong skill set over time, we will have multiple opportunities to showcase them, make changes as per the situation and succeed. On the flip side, if someone starts with a weak skill set and is not willing to improve it, time will only make things worse. They may try to fake intelligence or success for some time, not forever.

Hence, we (as individuals or as companies) should constantly observe what happens to us over time. We should strive to use time as our friend and improve, achieve bigger and better things. If time happens to make us worse, it is a signal that we must introspect and find out how to get our basics right. Once this is taken care of, time will suddenly become our friend.

☑ **The Warren Lesson:** ***Time is your friend if you have good basics.***

9

Income and Consumptions

Personal Finance is an essential skill that everyone needs. But, it is rarely taught to individuals in a structured manner. Everyone learns it in different ways, mostly by trial and error, making expensive mistakes and learning lessons from them.

For example, living within our means looks very obvious but it is not that easy. There are lifestyle choices that have increased the number of our needs and the corresponding salary or income is not able to catch up with them. As a result, people use tools such as loans or side hustles to somehow fill this gap and pay their bills.

While these are useful tools, they come with a cost. People can easily fall into the debt trap or have no time to spend with their friends and families, on their passions and hobbies due to overworking.

Warren Buffett gives one simple rule for personal finance: you should always adjust your consumption to your income, and not your income to your consumption. This means, always look at what your inputs are and decide on your outputs accordingly and don't let your outputs decide what your inputs should be. This helps in setting the right expectations for ourselves and avoids disappointments.

This lesson is applicable for individuals as well as companies, organisations, and even countries. All these have income streams and consumption streams and it is important that they are not out of sync.

What if you want to improve your consumption? For example, what if one wants to drive a better car or live in a better house or have an expensive vacation every few months?

These are fair demands and people can always get there. But, instead of using shortcuts and hurrying to these large consumption goals, it makes sense for them to watch the current state of their income and arrive at scaled-down consumption goals. Now, these will be met comfortably without any pain as they have already matched income and consumption. As their income grows, corresponding consumption goals can get larger and larger. This is a healthy pattern that ensures the best of both worlds.

Of course, this doesn't mean people should consume everything they earn. There is also a need for savings and intelligent investments which made Warren of today.

☑ **The Warren Lesson:** ***Always adjust your Consumption to your Income, not your Income to your Consumption.***

10

What does a Leader Really do?

Every company has two kinds of people: leaders and workers.

As the names suggest, leaders lead and workers work. But, such a one-dimensional view can hide us from the fact that leaders also work. They perform an important task that others in the organisation don't (and many times can't): seeing where their company or team should be and boldly taking other people there.

Why does this need boldness?

Many times, the path seen by the leaders (in their mind) is not easy or already tried. However, they see a reason to walk that difficult path and lead others there so that the benefits can be realised. When they are bold, others trust them and follow them.

Warren Buffett says, a leader should have visions and goals for a company for a long time horizon. But, this is only the first part of the puzzle, just having the right vision is not enough, they should also achieve them through other people. They should influence others to walk in the direction they take them and use their skills for the greater benefit of everyone.

Hence, true leaders will never feel insecure about their subordinates being more skilled or intelligent than them. In fact, they will make it a habit to hire such people in their team because accomplishing the vision is an equally important task and you need more hands and brains to make it happen.

Organisations typically have a hierarchy of leaders. Someone at the top thinks about the whole group's vision and future; a few people under him/her think about the vision and future of individual companies; more people under them think about the vision and future of specific groups or teams. Irrespective of level, all of them have a common aspect which is seeing into the future and leading others. In addition, they also spot leaders in their teams, coach them to do the same at a different level. This is how companies grow.

A small version of such a system runs inside all individuals too. We all have a vision or goal for ourselves and we get them accomplished through our own performance. This means we are our own leaders and our own workers. It helps in our personal growth.

☑ **The Warren Lesson:** ***Leaders should have Visions and Goals, and they should achieve them through other people.***

11

Best Salespeople

Businesses deploy a variety of sales and marketing techniques to inform and attract potential customers. They go door to door talking about their products and services, demonstrate their creations to customers, give huge discounts and offers, use huge billboards to talk about their features and benefits, publish multicolour advertisements in newspapers and magazines, run cool video advertisements in television channels and websites, use affiliates to bring new customers and so on. There are sales, marketing experts all over the globe and these fields are constantly growing and thriving.

However, when it comes to truly winning a customer, "Satisfied customers are a store's best salespeople", says Warren Buffett. Treat your customer well, give them a high-quality product at the right price, service them right and ensure the customer gets the full value and they will automatically become your salespeople. They will happily go and tell others about the great value you provided and people trust such feedback much more than the paid advertisements.

Of course, this doesn't mean other sales and marketing efforts are useless. Many of the companies, where Warren has invested, spend millions of dollars every year on advertisements and other ways to bring in a customer to their store or to make them pick their products. But, all those are useful only when the store or the product satisfies their need. That's the core advantage that actually converts someone interested to a real customer.

Similarly, when Warren appears in stage shows and television interviews and talks about his company and the businesses where he has invested, he also acts as a great advertiser and salesperson. However, it works only because what he does (value investing) works and creates wealth for others. People who invested in his company are happy and they act as salespeople and tell others.

Whatever be our business or industry, the focus should entirely be on our customer's needs and expectations. Understanding them, solving their problems and satisfying them, should be our first priority. When it happens, they go and tell others and success follows naturally.

☑ **The Warren Lesson:** ***Satisfied Customers are the best Salespeople.***

12

The "Easy" Way to Make Mistakes

When you look at a viral tweet or video, there are hundreds (sometimes thousands) of comments. Some of them are genuine appreciations or criticisms. But some of those comments don't seem to make any sense. Many people just seem to be adding all sorts of things in their mind as comments, whether they are relevant to the current discussion or not. If those people faced the same tweet or video situation in real life, they probably wouldn't react like that. But, while they are online, they do it not once, not twice, but multiple times. They repeat the unusual behaviour again and again. What could be the reason?

"Ease of doing something makes people do things that don't make a lot of sense", says Warren Buffet. When something has a low entry barrier and can be done easily without thinking, people just seem to do that: they shake their shoulders with a casual 'why not?' and do it!

On the flip side, when something is slightly difficult or has a higher entry barrier, it makes people stop and think. That brief pause filters out some nonsense habits.

For example, if money grows on trees and can be earned by anyone easily, people are less likely to have saving habits or disciplined spending habits. But, if one has to work hard to earn it, he/she will think twice before spending it away on something useless.

Being a great investor, Warren uses a stock market example to explain this, "Buying businesses on wall street is so easy. You can buy one at 10:00 and sell it at 10:05. But most of the fortunes were made in relatively few securities and ones that were held for a very long time and one that the buyer understood."

In this example, Warren shows both the easy way and hard way of owning a business. The easy way happens with a click of a button and you don't need to know anything about a company. As long as you have money, you can buy a business without thinking.

But the hard way involves understanding the business before making a decision. You may still click a button to buy this business too, but you are not doing it because the button exists, you are doing it after careful analysis.

The modern world with its technical innovations is making things easier than ever. Just because we can e-mail or text anyone anytime, we shouldn't let that low barrier of entry make us do things that don't make sense. An easy tool needs tremendous self-control on the part of the user.

☑ **The Warren Lesson:** ***Just because something is easy to do, don't forget to think before doing it.***

13

Being a Complete Leader

Everyone knows Warren Buffett is a great investor. But, what does he invest in?

Of course, he buys stocks of companies, sometimes buying entire companies. However, 'company' or 'business' is a very generic term and it becomes meaningful only when we consider what value it brings to the table: it may be a great product or a service or a brand recognition or a social impact or a wonderful team that understands the industry and runs the business well.

When making his investment decisions, Warren always looks at the people behind the business. This is because almost all the time he lets those people continue running their business as always, even after it changes hands. As he has a variety of businesses under his investment umbrella, he needs such experts and gives them a free hand to operate.

In one of his shareholder letters, Warren describes what skills his team looks at when hiring directors for their companies:

- Business-savvy
- Owner-oriented
- Strong specific interest in our company
- Actions guided by thoughts and principles, not robot-like processes
- Seeking managers who delight their customers, cherish their associates and act as good citizens to communities and countries.

This list shows the holistic expectations that Warren has in an executive: they should understand business, care for the owners and bring them value; they should be truly interested in the company and not just be motivated by money or other extrinsic motivations alone; they should be original thinkers; they should build a team of managers who keep customer satisfaction, employee satisfaction at the centre of everything they do while doing their bit to people around them.

Some may consider this to be an "impossible list". But, these expectations are not items that you study in a college or learn by working in a company for many years. They are solid foundations that make people complete leaders, they drive their thought process, controlling every decision they make. This culture fit is important and can take the company (and individuals) to great heights.

☑ **The Warren Lesson:** ***Be a complete leader.***

14

Margin of Safety

Let us say, you have a truck that weighs 9,800 pounds. You are driving this truck on one side of a river and your destination is on the other side. You are looking for a bridge that can help you cross it.

Suddenly, you see a bridge. It says, "Capacity: 10,000 pounds."

Now, will you drive your truck over that bridge?

Technically, the bridge's capacity is above the weight of your truck. So, it should be safe to drive the truck over it. But, you normally don't do that. Instead, you will continue driving until you find another bridge that says, "Capacity: 15,000 pounds". Now you happily drive your truck over that bridge.

If you go purely by the numbers, the first bridge is as good as the second bridge because your truck's weight is lower than both their capacities. Yet, the second bridge gives us additional comfort because it has a higher "margin of safety". This means, if something goes wrong in the first bridge and the capacity calculation is wrong by a small margin, you are likely to face a problem. This is less likely to happen in the second bridge because it has a higher margin of safety.

When Warren Buffett analyses a company, he looks at two important factors: the price at which he might buy the company and the company's value estimate. If there is a small gap between them, he normally doesn't invest in that company, unless and until there is some other strong reason to do so. This is because the margin of safety is so low, it doesn't accommodate possible errors in his analysis.

The margin of safety is an important factor not just in investment decisions, but in our everyday decisions as well. For example, if you are preparing for a 15 minutes speech, you must have enough material to cover 25 minutes, because it will take care of possible errors in your "number of words per minute" calculations.

When observed carefully, almost every decision can be enhanced by identifying the equivalent of those two magic numbers: the truck's weight and the bridge's capacity. If the gap between them is small, better find another bridge (or switch to a smaller truck).

☑ **The Warren Lesson:** ***When making decisions, have enough Margin of Safety to accommodate unknowns.***

15

Be Your Own Compliance Officer

Large organisations have their own compliance departments. Officers in this department look at various operations of that organisation and ensure that they are always complying with the applicable laws. If they see a problem, they immediately raise an alarm and ensure that it is corrected.

But, what drives this process? Are companies doing this because they are afraid of the law and possible punishment for misbehaviour? Are they doing this because the government will be angry if they don't? Or, are they doing this because they genuinely want to do the right thing and are not interested in making money by the wrong means?

Warren Buffett asks his employees and associates to ask a simple question before engaging in any act: if this appears in the local newspaper tomorrow and is read by everyone I love, will I still do it?

This question can convert each one of us into our own compliance officers. We will think about the act from a new perspective and will start skipping shortcuts. It will motivate us to do the right thing even when no one is watching and it will make us feel good.

For example, these days we hear a lot about cheating in online interviews. Some people do all sorts of tricks to land a job that they may not deserve. They may even consider themselves clever for doing so and laugh at their friends who are failing.

But, while the result is important, the means used to arrive there, are equally important. Someone cheating their way to a great job opening or a business deal or an election victory breaks this natural law. They may feel happy at that moment and enjoy the glory, but their own heart won't forgive them for getting there using unfair means.

"We've got all the money we need. [But,] we don't have an ounce of reputation beyond what we need and we can't afford to lose it", declares Warren. "We never will trade reputation away for money."

That's why Warren and many other leaders insist on integrity as an essential value. If you can't look at the mirror and say 'I did the right thing today', all the success in the world is meaningless.

☑ ***The Warren Lesson: If your actions appears in a local newspaper tomorrow and is read by everyone you love, will you still do it?***

16

Tails and Legs

Joseph was eating a chocolate bar which surprised Nancy. "I thought you were on a diet", she exclaimed.

"Yes, I am", answered Joseph.

"But, now you are eating a chocolate bar."

"Yes. But, Chocolate is made from cocoa beans. Hence, I call this a Salad", told Joseph, taking a big bite.

We all know a chocolate bar is not a salad. Joseph also knows it. But, he decides to call it a Salad so that he can stick to his diet. It may make him happy but won't get the results one expects from a diet.

Warren Buffett uses a riddle from Abraham Lincoln to explain such a thought process, "If you call a dog's tail a leg, how many legs does it have?"

Contrary to popular belief, the answer is not five. Just because we call a tail a leg, it doesn't become one. A dog still has four legs and one tail, irrespective of the different labels you use.

Warren quotes this example to laugh at questionable practices from some organisations that cleverly label their costs as something else so that the final numbers look 'good'. But, this is just an illusion and doesn't become a fact.

When we are facing difficult problems which can't be solved, an easy way out can be labelling them in a different way. For example, someone who spends a lot of time on Facebook may call it "relax time" or "me time" or even declare that the Facebook feed is an information source. Such a change in the label is convenient because we don't have to change the status quo, yet, claim that we have achieved what we wanted to. But it will be a false victory.

Hence, it may be a good practice to question our beliefs. We may be under an illusion or we may be believing something because that's how it was always presented to us by our parents or teachers or seniors. Just because we always called a tail as a leg or a chocolate bar as a salad, it doesn't become one. Asking this question and understanding reality can make us see the world better and improve our thinking and actions.

☑ **The Warren Lesson:** ***Face Reality.***

17

Circle of Competence

Warren Buffett may be one of the best investors the world has seen. But, that doesn't mean he spotted and made use of every great opportunity in the stock market. There are many companies where he didn't invest, but they went on to become great successes. Does that bother him?

Yes and No. If a company is outside his circle of evaluating competence and he missed to spot its potential success, he is not worried. But, if something is within his circle of competence and he missed spotting it, he realises that as a big mistake and learns from it.

This term (circle of competence) may be new to many. But, it is familiar to us and we all have our own circles of competence in various matters. Let us understand this with an example.

Warren is an expert in understanding businesses in certain industries. If there is a company that he wants to invest in and it falls in one of those industries, he can read about the company and understand it better to make the right decision. He may decide to invest or skip the opportunity. His decision may be right or wrong. But in either case, it will be a calculated move because he understands this business.

However, there are other industries that Warren doesn't understand well. When there is an opportunity in one of those industries, he sees it as falling outside his circle of competence because he can't understand the business to make a decision.

We need to remember that this circle needn't remain constant. Warren can always learn about new industries and expand his circle of competence. But, his success is not determined by the size of this circle. Even if he has a small circle, he can still be a big winner by taking the right calls within that small circle, ignoring the areas outside.

The circle of competence is not specific to the share market or investment world. Every individual creates his/her own circle of competence in certain areas through education, experience and interest. They should understand the boundaries of this circle very well so that they can always play to their strengths.

☑ **The Warren Lesson:** ***Understand your circle of competence, especially its boundaries.***

18

Views of Others

Some people like hearing their own voice in any forum. They may have other experts and subordinates around, but their love for their personal thoughts prevents them from hearing the views of others and considering them before making a decision.

When seen logically, one person cannot be the expert on every topic and it is practically impossible for that one person to have all the skills, knowledge and experience. There is huge value in the diversity of thoughts that come when we listen to others. It gives us new perspectives, helps us form new connections in the brain. In addition, it also makes those other people feel good about their contribution in the decision-making.

However, Warren Buffett asks us to be careful about whose advice we listen to. He explains this with a piece of humorous advice, "Don't ask the barber whether you need a haircut."

As the barber benefits from every person who decides to go for a haircut, their opinion about whether someone needs a haircut or not is likely to be clouded by this interest. They may be honest people and tell you the truth most of the time, but why take that risk?

Hence, when we are thinking about a problem and want to explore it from multiple dimensions, collect various possible solutions, analyse them and arrive at the best course of action, we should expand our toolkit by speaking to others. But, we need to select them carefully in such a way that there is no conflict of interest and their views are likely to be balanced.

For example, if we want to buy a car, we can speak to an expert who analyses cars from various brands and can give us a balanced view. But, going to a particular brand's showroom and asking the salesperson there, is less likely to give us the right details. As this salesperson has a personal motivation to sell that car (or another car from that brand) to us, he is likely to exaggerate the benefits and downplay the issues. This doesn't mean we shouldn't talk to salespersons at all, but they shouldn't be the only sources for our decision-making. We need to take their views with a pinch of salt or verify them with facts.

☑ **The Warren Lesson:** ***Carefully select your advisors depending on each topic or problem.***

19

A Car you can't Replace

Everyone has a dream car. They may not be able to afford it immediately. But, they start from somewhere and progress towards their dream car steadily.

Hence, when it comes to buying a car, people may not hesitate to experiment. They tend to pick the car that they like at that moment and something they can afford. If things don't work well, they know they can sell it and go for a different car later.

Warren Buffett brings a twist to this usual habit and asks us to imagine that we can only buy one car in our lifetime. This means, there is no option to change it for another (hopefully) better car, and we need to drive it forever. If we lose it, we can't buy a new car. In such a situation, imagine how much care we will show towards that single car and how gently we will take care of it!

Through this interesting thought exercise, Warren teaches us an important lesson: Our Body and Mind are not replaceable.

They are not cars that you can change if you are unhappy with them or if they have some problems. They are like the only car that we will have forever. Hence, we need to take good care of them so that they serve us well into our ripe old age.

In today's use and throw culture, we attach very little sentiment to any object because they can be easily replaced as long as we can afford a new one. Hence, we tend to mistreat or misuse them without thinking. Unfortunately, the same habit gets in even in the way we treat our body and mind: we don't think twice about eating unhealthy food or compromising on necessary sleep to get something done. These may look like good choices now, but if and when we need to replace the car, we will come to know that it can't be replaced. At that time, we will feel bad about our life choices. That's precisely the point Warren makes: don't wait till the point of no return, take good care of your body and mind now as they can't be replaced; give them the attention that they deserve.

☑ **The Warren Lesson:** ***Your Body and Mind are precious assets. Take good care of them.***

20
The Perfect Choice

In 1986, Warren Buffett interviewed someone for an insurance-related position. He asked the young man, "What experience do you have in the insurance domain?"

He replied, "None."

Usually, such an answer will result in a rejection. After all, the position needs insurance domain experience and what is the point in hiring someone who has no experience in that domain?

But, for some reason, Warren didn't consider it as a strong reason to reject this person. He saw some other qualities and decided to hire him with the note that 'Nobody's perfect.'

That young man whom Warren hired in 1986 is Ajit Jain, currently the Vice Chairman of Insurance Operations for Warren's Berkshire Hathaway. Someone who had no experience whatsoever in the insurance domain, went on to become a great asset for Warren's organisation and an industry leader driving big growth and profits.

Today, Warren calls Ajit the 'perfect choice' for that position and openly praises Ajit in multiple forums. But, many human resource experts may not agree with him. They might argue that this is a lucky selection and it could've easily gone the other way. Hence, they conclude that hiring should be strictly based on factors such as skills and experience that the candidate has.

Agreed, hiring someone shouldn't be a random process and it helps if the candidate has the right skills and experience. But, this focus shouldn't result in a machine-like selection process that expects perfection ignoring many other strengths that the candidates might be bringing to the table. For example, Warren saw something in Ajit which made him ignore Ajit's lack of experience in the insurance domain and trust him to do that job well. You can't teach this to a machine and expect it to take the right call. We are human beings and we see other human beings holistically and make decisions. This is true not just for hiring decisions, but also various other decisions such as whom to interact with, whom to do business with, where to study, whom to marry and so on.

Hence, when interacting with someone new, we should keep both channels open: the brain channel which looks at data and matches them with our needs and expectations as well as the heart channel which looks beyond data and thinks what else is important and useful in working with that individual. Balancing these two during decision making and constantly learning from the results of such decisions can help us become better thinkers and decision-makers.

☑ **The Warren Lesson: *Look at People Holistically.***

21
Dealing with Bad Decisions

When we buy a pack of biscuits or a cool drink, we don't have to think much about the price to pay. Manufacturers of those products clearly specify their retail price and we need to just pay it, minus any discount. Easy!

But, buying a business is a different story. No business comes with a price tag. It has to be calculated based on various factors, including but not limited, to the value that the business brings. Hence, investors do a lot of calculations before arriving at the right price. Even then, there is no assurance that the price is right. Only time can tell, that is, only the future performance of that business will indicate whether they have paid too little or too much for it.

Warren Buffett is known as an expert in assessing companies. But, he too makes mistakes and talks openly about them. His letters to stockholders regularly contain such revelations.

But, when Warren talks about paying too much for a business, there is no regret in his voice. This is not because he wants to throw away money. In fact, he is one of the biggest advocates of paying the right price (or better, a discounted price) and calls himself a bargain-hunter. Still, he is not worried about paying too much for a business because such things get adjusted over time even though there are some short-term impacts.

For example, he might have paid too much for a business which can result in an immediate bottom-line impact for his company. But, over time, the business performs well or other businesses where Warren has invested hit gold and things get balanced. As this is always a possibility, there is no point in getting worried too much about a single bad decision.

Of course, we should give every decision the attention it deserves. But, if things don't go well, despite this, we needn't be too hard on ourselves. Either accept it as an error, take the learnings and move on or wait for the time to balance out things. Chill!

☑ **The Warren Lesson:** ***When you have a structured thinking process for decision-making, don't worry about decisions that go wrong now and then. Don't be too hard on yourself for them and move on.***

22

Possibilities: Good and Bad

Let us say someone is telling you about a potential problem that might occur a few years down the line. If it happens, it is a big problem and can create huge issues for yourself and the people around you. But, if it doesn't happen, you can relax. Unfortunately, you don't know whether it is going to happen or not with any certainty because you are not an expert in that domain. In such a situation, what will you do?

Warren Buffett faced a similar situation when someone asked him to consider the Climate Change problem and its possible impact on his insurance business. Will he do anything differently now because Climate Change can cause some disruptions in the future?

"I have no scientific aptitude", responded Warren, "However, it would be foolish for me or anyone to demand 100% proof of forthcoming damage to the world if that outcome seemed at all possible and if prompt action had even a small chance of thwarting the danger."

This means, even though we can't say for sure that a dangerous situation is going to occur in a certain number of years, we still need to take action now because of a simple calculation: magnitude of benefits that can occur if we act now Vs magnitude of losses we might face if we don't act now. "If there is only a 1% chance the planet is heading towards a truly major disaster and delay means passing a point of no return, inaction now is foolhardy", declares Warren.

We may not face Climate Change level problem possibilities in our everyday life. But, we regularly come across "important, but not urgent now" tasks that we tend to delay in favour of "urgent" tasks. When doing so, we need to remember the thought process Warren teaches us when thinking about Climate Change: is there a slim chance that this delay (or a series of such delays) can cause a point of no return in future? If yes, is this delay a wise decision?

For example, someone might regularly delay starting an exercise routine because they are constantly busy with many other things. When they think about the slim (no pun intended) chance of a big health issue in future, they may understand that not acting now is unacceptable. Instead of arguing 'what is the exact probability or proof of this health issue occurring to me?', they will think about the benefits of assuming, that is going to happen in future and taking concrete action now.

☑ **The Warren Lesson:** ***If there is a small chance of a big problem occurring in future, opt for 'action' against 'inaction' now, as long as the benefits of 'action' are considerably large.***

23

Best Person for the Job

Every year, hundreds and thousands of people are entering the job market with the belief that the system respects their talent, looks at their potential and gives them the right opportunities to grow. In return, they are ready to work hard and help the organisation that trusts them with the opportunity.

While 'best person for the job' is rightfully the norm that is driving any industry, there are instances where we see people using back doors to enter a job position. They may use their relationship with one of the existing team members or any other influence to get there. When such a route is taken by someone unqualified, other qualified candidates waiting for an opportunity are disappointed. In addition, this also hurts the organisation because the best person is not selected for the job which will reflect in the quality of work and results. It can spread negative energy in the team because talented people will start questioning whether they will have a fair chance to grow in this organisation.

"Meritocracy is important", says Warren Buffet. He explains this with a beautiful example: when a country is picking people for its Olympics team, they go for the best athletes and players, not sons or daughters of previous medal winners.

Of course, sons or daughters of previous medal winners may be great players and they can enter the Olympics team by showing their skills and talent; they can enter there by consistently winning many competitions and showing that they belong to the country's topmost players list. As long as no one enters there for just being the child of a previous winner or by knowing a senior official, the competition is fair.

Similarly, when someone is selected for a job, whom a candidate knows or who recommends that candidate should never be a category. Even someone with no connections whatsoever should be able to get that position as long as he/she is best qualified for that position. This keeps a level playing ground and helps the organisation also by creating a healthy environment for everyone to contribute and succeed.

☑ **The Warren Lesson*: Respect Meritocracy.***

24

The Selection Criteria

Warren Buffett's Berkshire Hathaway owns many businesses, some of them fully and many others partially. These companies range from candy makers to insurance providers to railway lines. A casual look into the list of companies owned by Berkshire Hathaway may make one wonder if there is any logic at all in that compilation. They may even conclude that Warren and his friend and partner, Charlie Munger just buy businesses randomly.

But, the truth is far from this assumption. Berkshire Hathaway is so successful because the companies it owns, are not selected randomly. Warren and Charlie carefully pick them based on various rules. In fact, they don't even keep those rules a secret. They have published it as an open "Berkshire Hathaway Acquisition Criteria", inviting businesses to come and talk to them if their business meets the given criteria:

1. Large Purchases
2. Demonstrated Consistent Earning Power
3. Good Returns on Equity; Little or No Debt
4. Management in Place
5. Simple Businesses
6. An Offering Price.

When we read this acquisition criteria, the first thing that strikes us is its simplicity. There is no ambiguity in which acquisitions Berkshire Hathaway is interested in and which acquisitions they are not interested in. Any business can easily tick (or not tick) these six boxes and conclude whether they should call Warren's office or not.

Similarly, when someone calls Warren's office about a possible acquisition, it is very easy for the office staff to decide whether this is a conversation worth pursuing or not. For example, as Warren himself explains, if a transaction's price is unknown, Berkshire Hathaway is not interested in any further discussions, even preliminary ones.

Hence, a simple criteria definition helps both parties think clearly and avoid unnecessary wastage of time. Bringing such clarity to a complex topic such as acquisition, teaches us the importance of keeping the rules simple: when everyone knows the criteria, there is no ambiguity and a lot of progress.

This lesson can be applied in multiple scenarios such as hiring someone for a job (or applying for a job), picking the right projects to focus on, identifying the right social cause to donate money or time etc. When we make the criteria clear, decision-making becomes easy and less error-prone.

> ☑ **The Warren Lesson:** ***When you have to make a decision, first clearly define your selection criteria.***

25

Making People Listen to You

A stranger approaches you at a party. He extends his hand with a warm smile and introduces himself. You don't know him, but still, you talk to him because he looks friendly. After all, parties are places where you make new friendships, isn't it?

However, within the next few minutes, you lose interest in this person, looking around the room for an excuse to move away. Why? He starts talking about his company or the new product that he sells and directly or indirectly asks you to buy from him. This makes it clear that he originally contacted you not for friendship, but only for business.

The same behaviour can be seen online too. Many of the new people who friend you or follow you on social media approach you with a business proposal in no time. When this happens, your fingers immediately rush to the "unfollow" or "block" button.

In general, people are not afraid of new friendships, they are not even against the idea of giving business to someone. But, they dislike fake friendships created with the only purpose of selling something to them.

Warren Buffett owns many companies whose products and services he is proud of. In his interviews, he frequently mentions these companies, their products and services and encourages people to go and buy from them. In fact, he himself is a walking billboard of his companies.

Yet, people listen to Warren; they take his advice seriously. Every interview, every stage appearance of him is followed by thousands and thousands of people eagerly. When he hosts a Q&A session, people are lining up to ask their questions and hear his opinions. What could be the reason?

"I am not selling them anything", says Warren Buffett, "[What I am giving them is] just an unbiased advice from somebody who's been around a long time. It worked for me. I try to talk their language. I think people can tell when you are saying what you believe versus talking points."

This is a fantastic advice on how to talk so that people listen. While Warren explicitly talks about his companies, products and services now and then, he doesn't let this bias the opinions he shares or his genuine advice to someone. He believes in telling the truth, telling them something that he himself tried and succeeded (or failed). He only shares what he truly believes, and doesn't carry talking points that generally focus only on pleasing the audience. This means, he may even share unpopular opinions sometimes, but that's only because he believes them. When someone is truthful, others can see it and they respect it.

So, if you run a company and approach someone new, should you not talk about your business to them?

Of course, you can. But, make it a genuine consultation which benefits both the parties. First, understand their problem(s) and see whether your solution is suitable to solve their problem(s). If yes, explain why you believe your offering will work for them, along with its possible weaknesses. Finally, let them take the call based on the suitability, quality and price of your offering. By doing this, you are moving away from a blind sales pitch to unbiased advice which helps both of you.

☑ **The Warren Lesson:** ***Give unbiased advice and people will listen.***

26

Don't Teach a Fish How to Swim

When Berkshire Hathaway acquires a company, they usually retain the same senior leadership to run the business exactly the same way they did before the acquisition. Warren Buffett doesn't believe in giving 'instructions' to those managers and leaders on how to run their business, because they were doing it for many years and were successful, why interfere with that?

Given Warren's stature and track record in running successful companies, leaders of those companies may want to listen to him and give serious consideration to his thoughts. But, this can also backfire as they might attach too much value to his opinions because of his position. In addition, it can affect scalability as Warren can't be focusing on every business, trying to give high value strategic consulting or advice to all his leaders. Instead, by giving them the freedom to operate in their areas of expertise and providing an opinion only on matters where they need support,

Warren sets up their individual organisations and the Berkshire Hathaway group for success.

As a bonus, the trust, Warren keeps in these leaders, acts as tremendous motivation for them to perform better than ever. He openly praises them in multiple forums and acknowledges the value they bring to the table. He is one of those rare leaders who will be happy to say, "I don't know much about this particular business, it is totally handled by our leader of this company."

"If my job were to manage a golf team and if Jack Nicklaus or Arnold Palmer were willing to play for me, neither would get a lot of directives from me about how to swing", says Warren. We can see that this strategy works because many of the companies acquired by Berkshire Hathaway continue to remain successful, some of them growing multifold and getting better value than ever for shareholders.

Recognising talent, expertise and giving people the freedom to operate is an important trait for any leader. This attitude comes only when they are humble and accept the fact that they can't be experts in everything just because they have a large title. Different people come with different skills and a combination of all those is valuable for a company or a group. Everyone contributing with their thoughts is acceptable, but interfering with someone's job with our limited (or even amazing) knowledge can cause unnecessary friction. When a leader recognises this and trusts everyone to bring their best to the table, everyone gets the satisfaction of doing their best for the organisation.

☑ **The Warren Lesson:** ***Trust your leaders and give them the freedom to excel.***

27
Watch the Puck

Wayne Gretzky is a famous ice hockey player and coach from Canada. Warren Buffett quotes one of his sayings as a piece of investment advice, "Go where the puck is going, not where it is."

For the benefit of those who might not know, a puck is a hard rubber disk used in ice hockey games. Players constantly chase it so that their team can control it better. Hence, knowing the exact location of the puck in the ice rink at any given point of time is valuable information for every player.

Average players may just look at the puck and try to reach there so that they can play it. But, by the time they reach there, some other player might have moved it to a different location, forcing them to rethink their strategy. If this happens throughout the game, they will keep moving (to the place where the puck is), but will not impact the result of the game much.

Instead, if they invest in careful observation of the field, other players (from both teams), their positions, movements and the puck's current movement itself, they can stay a step ahead of everyone else and can reach where the puck is going. Of course, there is no assurance that they will be right every time, but this approach is better than reaching the current and transient location of the puck.

Warren considers Wayne's advice to be a useful tip when picking the right companies to invest in. But, the scope of this strategy moves beyond the investment world. Irrespective of the field we are operating in, we need to constantly invest in understanding the current way things are working, trends and the future direction where they are going. These predictions may not be accurate. But, by consciously thinking about where the puck is going, we are in a better position to handle various possibilities, including those that need course corrections from our side.

For example, a student learning to code can look at the current programming languages, their usage patterns, newly introduced technologies, languages, their pros and cons, adoption rates, success and failure of these in the hands of various small, medium and large companies etc which improves their chances of understanding where the programming puck goes. This knowledge will then lead to them investing time in the right technologies instead of being dependent on what everyone around them is learning.

But, this can't be a one time process. They should continue watching the trends to understand if the original assumptions they made are still valid; if they see some mismatches, they can quickly readjust the path to ensure their understanding of the puck's new location improves their chances of success. In today's constantly changing world, it pays to regularly understand where the puck is going next.

☑ **The Warren Lesson:** ***Instead of focusing on the puck's current location, go where the puck is going and invest your money or time there.***

28

Clear Boundaries

In today's world, most victorious individuals seem to give away something in return for their success. It could be health, sleep, exercise, family time, personal interests or something else... These are seen as costs of success that must be paid.

Once Warren Buffett was discussing a business deal and shared his proposal. He asked the other party to call him with their thoughts and indicated that they can proceed with the next steps if they show interest.

However, Warren asked this other party not to call him regarding this deal for the next few hours. Why? Because on that day he had plans to go out with his grandchildren and didn't want to be disturbed while he was spending quality time with them.

This incident may be dismissed as too old-style by modern entrepreneurs and leaders. They may argue, "if it is such an important deal, why make the other party wait? Just have fun with your family and when the call comes, excuse yourself, spend a minute or two to discuss the matter with the other party and close it. Easy!"

While multitasking is seen as an essential skill in the workplace and some people even use it to mix personal and official tasks together, multiple researches show that humans can't really multitask. It is just an illusion. Every time we think we are doing multiple things in parallel, we actually stop one and start the other rapidly. This stop, start process has its own cost which nullifies the effect of multitasking. We may be better off handling one task at a time to get maximum efficiency.

Similarly, Warren's example also shows the need to draw the boundaries between personal and professional time. It is okay to make an exception here and there in some circumstances; but, the moment we relax the rules too much and start allowing any sort of interruption anywhere, we will not enjoy both worlds.

Another important point is the message Warren sends to people around him by saying 'don't call me when I am spending time with my family'. It stresses the importance of work-life balance and encourages everyone to take it seriously. When a leader acts that way, others follow and it helps them excel professionally, while having a healthy personal life.

☑ **The Warren Lesson:** ***Enjoy your personal time fully. You can pick up business tasks when you are back!***

29

Don't Keep Scores

When two teams play a game, someone carefully keeps the score and updates it regularly. Hence, at any given point of time, you will know which team has scored how much, what the gap is and who is winning.

Even outside the sports world, people keep scores. For example, students may keep a score of the number of lessons they have studied, the number of topics they have revised, etc. Mountaineers may keep a list of mountains they have scaled and haven't scaled.

We should remember that not every score is noted down on a piece of paper or electronic scoreboard for everyone to see. Some scores may just be registered in the minds of people; yet, they remain as strong indicators of their performance and success, at least to themselves. They may also guide their next step as different kinds of scores will need different kinds of actions.

Don't Keep Scores

Keeping scores is good and many times motivates us to do better. However, the problem starts when people bring the same habit in a relationship, trying to keep a running score with their friends, family members, business partners, co-workers, etc.

For example, let us say a husband and wife are arguing about a certain decision to be taken. If both of them openly discuss the merits and demerits of the given options based on the available data, it will lead to a better conversation. Alternatively, what if one of them goes like this: "Your suggestions on these matters are always bad; let me give you a few examples where you made these stupid decisions..."

Such a comment is the result of a mental 'score' the husband (or the wife) has kept all these years. He/she has seen this relationship as a sports match and has noted down instances where they won and instances where the other party won. If the other party also kept a similar score, this becomes a faster downhill journey.

"You cannot keep score [in a relationship]", says Warren Buffett. "It just doesn't work with the best of human relationships."

What if we keep score in our minds and never express it to the other party?

According to Warren, it still doesn't work. We may implicitly indicate to the other party that we keep the score and that doesn't help enhance the relationship. "It shouldn't be even suppressed. It should be something that doesn't even exist."

This means that both parties should be open and understand that all of us make mistakes. Instead of keeping scores such as who said what, who's idea was finally selected, etc. The focus should be on having the right conversation considering all options so that the best option is arrived at collaboratively. Irrespective of who gave an idea, other people can enhance it with their thoughts, experience and expertise. In the short term, it improves the idea; in the long term, it strengthens the relationship.

Hence, when we work with other people in our personal or professional life, it is important to remember that it is not a game with a single winner and there is no use in keeping score. When we approach people with this mindset, we don't try to win or dominate that relationship, it becomes a two-way street where both people contribute happily.

☑ **The Warren Lesson:** ***Don't keep scores with people. Instead, have open conversations and help each other.***

30

Standard of Living

Cost of living is typically defined as the cost of maintaining a certain standard of living. For example, if you want to live in a comfortable house in a safe society, you need to spend a certain amount to buy or rent such a house. If you want a certain quality of food three times a day for all your family members, you need to pay for the ingredients, cooking fuel and energy to store food items safely. If you want to travel to your office with certain comforts, if you want your children to go to a private school, if you want to have an annual vacation in a foreign location, etc. all these add up to your total cost of living. Depending on whether your earnings/savings match or exceed this cost or not, you can enjoy all or some of them.

However, some people get this relationship wrong and assume that getting a very high income or accumulating a lot of wealth or assets automatically gives them a better, satisfying life.

While this is true to some extent, many researches suggest that once the basic needs are met, additional money doesn't increase life satisfaction. In fact, in many cases, the race and grind to earn that money can even reduce the feeling of satisfaction and happiness.

"Your standard of living is not equal to your cost of living", says Warren Buffett. Instead of calculating how much money we are able to bring to the table, we should start looking at what value it brings and what difference it makes.

For example, driving a cool, luxurious car to the office is wonderful. But, that doesn't mean those who use public transport or drive a smaller, less comfortable, less stylish car are having a rough life. They may be happy with their mode of transport and that's what matters.

Warren's life itself is a testimony to this advice. Even though he consistently features in the lists of richest people in the world, he is frugal, spends wisely and doesn't believe earning and spending money is the way to happiness.

☑ **The Warren Lesson:** ***Good standard of living doesn't mean spending a lot of money on everything. It comes from inner satisfaction.***

31
Working with Smart Customers

When Warren Buffett was young and looking for a job, he applied for an investment consultant job opening. During the interview, the interviewer asked him, "If you get this job, what kind of customers will you look for?"

"Smart customers", answered Warren. "They will understand what I'm talking about and they'll make money eventually [by the investments I am suggesting them.]."

"Wrong answer" declared the interviewer. "You should look for rich customers."

This interviewer's expectation is typical of conventional investment advisors of those days. They will look for rich people who can afford to spend money on large investments so that these advisors can make a lot of money through their commission for such investments.

But, Warren, even at that young age, didn't believe in this. He felt he should attract those customers who are smart, who can understand what he is doing, what he is suggesting and why he is suggesting it. Those customers tend to invest not because they have a lot of money, but because they believe in the strategy suggested by Warren. Hence, such customers tend to stick with him for the long term.

This is exactly what Warren did when he started his own business. Even today, those who invest in Berkshire Hathaway shares understand and trust Warren's methods and those are the kinds of customers he wants to work with.

Today's business world uses the term 'Velvet Rope Strategy' to describe the process of creating exclusivity with services or product offerings. In Warren's case, 'being a smart customer' and 'understanding my strategies and believing in them' were his velvet ropes. Those customers who crossed those velvet ropes benefitted the most. Warren also enjoys working with them.

In addition, Warren also managed to attract a large group of Smart Students. These students from all over the globe study Warren's methods so that they can understand them, customise them and use them in a way that makes sense for them. Warren may not get to work with all of them directly, but he has created these Smart Investors in every generation which continues even now.

When we trust in the intelligence of our customers, we are forced to provide something of true value. Fake promises won't work with them simply because they are smart. So, we need to work hard, improve our processes, offerings and as a result, we grow and succeed. It is a true win-win for everyone.

☑ **The Warren Lesson:** ***Work with smart customers.***

32

Products that Travel Well

One of my friends wrote a great business guide. It was accepted by a publisher and released as a beautiful paperback book. It sold well and got nice reviews too. This made my friend very happy.

A few months later, my friend got an email from a foreign publisher. They heard about the book and wanted to publish the same in their native language. My friend gave the necessary permission and within a few months, the book was released in a foreign language which my friend doesn't even know.

The story didn't stop there. The second language publication of the book made it even more popular and it got published in two other languages, all within the first year of publication.

I asked my friend whether he expected such a success for his book in four languages spoken in different parts of the world. He just laughed, "Well, I didn't. But, when I think retrospectively, it makes sense. The topic I chose was not a local one. It was understood and appreciated by people of different cultures and hence, I could use my one-time investment (researching and writing a book) to get multifold returns. If I chose a local topic, this wouldn't have happened."

When investing, Warren Buffett applies similar thinking and looks for products that 'travel well.' This means products that are not restricted to a specific market but can be successful in other markets too. For example, a soft drink or a chewing gum will travel well and can be manufactured, marketed and sold to a variety of markets and consumers. He likes investing in those products and in companies manufacturing such products because their market can grow beyond geographical boundaries and they can bring in more money than products that are locally successful but don't travel well.

We can apply Warren's idea when picking our projects or when deciding where to spend our time. If there are two tasks and one will have a larger, wider impact than the other, it may be wise to spend time on it so that we can maximise our returns. The other task can be either dropped or delegated or improved in such a way that it too has a wider impact.

☑ **The Warren Lesson:** ***Focus on products that travel well.***

33
The Path to Expertise

Every field has novices and experts. Both their behaviours and results are entirely different. After all, experts have years, sometimes decades, of learning experience with best practices embedded in all their actions. They seem to look at patterns that others totally miss; their decision-making is (usually) flawless, and even if they make a mistake, they are able to recover from it and course-correct smoothly. They learn lessons from those mistakes, implement those learnings and ensure it strengthens their overall performance. Hence, it is not easy for novices or even mini-experts to match them.

However, this shouldn't be a reason for non-experts to avoid entering that field altogether. Even those experts would've started somewhere and got here. Hence, they should remove the hesitation and enter the field, learn and improve. As the famous saying goes, you can't edit a blank page!

Warren Buffett is an investment expert. But, he tells others that "you don't have to be an expert in order to achieve satisfactory investment returns". In such scenarios, that is, when we are not an expert in what we are doing, he advises us to follow two simple rules:

First, we should recognise our limitations. Just like we know what we know, we should also know what we don't know. When this understanding is clear, we will look for ways to bridge this gap and minimise our damage possibilities.

"Unsophisticated investor who is realistic about his shortcomings is likely to obtain better long term results than the knowledgeable professional who is blind to even a single weakness", says Warren. Even though his observation is about the world of investing, it applies to every field and knowing our weaknesses is key to making the right decisions.

Second, we should identify and follow a course that is certain to work reasonably well. No one can predict the future accurately, but finding a path that has the maximum possibilities of things going well is doable and that's something a non-expert should look for.

These two rules may not guarantee success. But, they minimise risks and send us in the right direction. We should continue to observe, learn and improve. This smart path will make us experts in our chosen field.

☑ **The Warren Lesson:** ***When you are not an expert, recognise your limitations; follow a course certain to work reasonably well.***

34
Learning from Friends

How do we pick friends?

Some friendships start very early, from school days or even earlier. They may be people with whom we like to play or study or work or simply to talk nonstop. After that, we keep adding friends to our list as we grow. We may also remove friends from this list, but new ones keep coming to ensure a steady supply. These friends share our dreams, goals, feelings, anxieties, disappointments, expectations and secrets. From a small kid to an elderly person, everyone seems to need friends and enjoy their company.

But, is there any common thread that connects all these friendships?

"I learn from all my friends", says Warren Buffett. "It is difficult for me to be friends with someone from whom I don't learn something. That's the fun of having friends."

While we have a good time with our friends in a playground or classroom or office or theatre, we constantly learn from them. Some of them teach us good habits, best practices to be followed in different circumstances. A few others teach us what habits to avoid for us to succeed. They do this by talking, by sharing their experiences, by expressing their views about things they saw or heard, by demonstrating values through their behaviours and by openly providing us feedback on our actions.

Feedbacks coming from friends are most important because they are more likely to tell us the truth instead of sugar-coating it. They do this because they want us to succeed, they want us to grow, they want the world to look at us with awe and they want to enjoy that pride of being "the best pal of a successful person". When such feedback is shared reciprocally, both friends benefit and the bond between them strengthens.

Warren has explained in multiple forums how he enjoys working with his long time friend Charlie Munger. This is not because they always share niceties and agree with each other. They do have disagreements and some of Warren's decisions are challenged by Charlie. However, he doesn't take it personally because he knows that Charlie is a true friend and he respects his intelligence. This makes him reevaluate his original thought process and apply the perspective from Charlie. Hence, every disagreement becomes a learning opportunity.

When we have friends with varied skills and talents, we can constantly observe them and learn from them. This will be more effective than the learnings we get from classrooms, textbooks and preachings because it comes with fun and from people whom we love.

☑ **The Warren Lesson:** ***Learn from your friends.***

35

Prescriptive Approach vs. Descriptive Approach

Howard Buffett, the father of Warren Buffett, was a Congressman. He gave his son a terrific gift.

What was it? Money? Stocks? Lessons on Personal Finance? Contacts of his wealthy friends? Recommendation letter to a famous company?

All these would've been great gifts. But the gift Howard gave his son was even better and long-lasting: He told his son that he cared only about the values he had, not the particular path he chose.

This means Howard was not concerned about Warren trying something different from all others. He didn't want his son to follow a certain path simply because everyone else was doing it or because the chances of success are higher there. Howard believed that Warren will be successful in life as long as he has the right value system.

Warren says that his father told this to him both verbally and by behaviour. Howard informed his son that he had unlimited confidence in him and he should follow his dreams.

A typical parent today might be horrified to hear this. They may wonder what the kids know about life and its different paths and the things they would need to be successful. This may make them think that they need to instruct their children and guide them in the right direction, carefully watch their progress and do the necessary course corrections until they are ready. This would in turn lead to them pushing their own dreams on their children, influencing their choice of college or degree or job or anything else.

However, all this ‘guidance’ doesn’t guarantee success or happiness. Even if it does, the children will only be living their parents’ lives, not their own.

Compared to this, the route taken by Howard is pleasant and gives complete freedom to children, as long as their value systems are right. After all, it is their life and they should make the decisions. Parents can be there to give support if necessary, otherwise, set the basics right and let them explore the world.

This might apply even in a professional setting. When seniors start using a prescriptive approach (telling people what to do and how to do it) instead of a descriptive approach (telling people what needs to be done and letting them decide how to do it), their subordinates tend to become their poor copies or get frustrated and leave. Instead, if seniors give the right guidelines and give freedom to juniors to perform in a way they feel right, they may make mistakes, but will learn from them and grow to be better individuals.

☑ **The Warren Lesson:** ***Give your children (or subordinates) a terrific gift: care about their values, not the path they select.***

36

When it is Raining Gold...

Opportunities don't follow a regular pattern. They tend to arrive at a time when people least expect them, and they tend to vanish very fast, giving no room for those who hesitate.

Hence, everyone in any field should make 'looking for opportunities' a daily job. They should find systems and sources to search for opportunities, build intelligence to spot them early and act fast.

For example, a business owner operating in a certain field should continue watching the local and international markets, trends in customer behaviour, the performance of his/her competitors, partners and complementing services etc. If possible, they can have their own think tank which enhances their chances of spotting the right opportunity at the right time.

"Not using a right opportunity is a mistake", warns Warren Buffett. "Using it on a small scale and not grabbing it fully is also a mistake."

For example, if the business owner spots an opportunity for a great business relationship, he/she should also understand its full scale. It could be the dollar value of the opportunity or the number and depth of relationships it can create. While even a partial involvement will get great returns, if it is clear that the opportunity is a good one, it makes sense to use it fully. Warren explains it with a beautiful illustration, "when it is raining gold, reach for a bucket, not a thimble."

Another important aspect of using opportunities fully is being ready for them. Starting our preparation after the opportunity is spotted might be too late and the opportunity may not wait until we are fully ready. Hence, we should be ready to grab great opportunities when they arrive and this needs preparation of skills and resources. A business owner willing to use an international opportunity to expand his/her business should already have the right systems in place to discuss, close and get started with the necessary formalities even before the opportunity is spotted. While doing so, we need to make sure that we prepare a bucket for the gold rain, even though there is not a single drop in sight yet.

☑ ***The Warren Lesson: Spot the right opportunities, and use them fully.***

37

What Makes a Product Great?

There are hundreds of thousands of product companies all around us. Starting from the toothpaste we use in the morning to the mobile phone we carry everywhere to the car we drive, we use and endorse multiple products and companies that make them.

But, except for the fact that they all make products, these companies are not the same. Their size and degree of success vary a lot. Some products attract customers (and repeat customers) easily, selling in large numbers, while other products need to struggle, make some noise before they can make any sale.

If you are an investor (or a business owner), companies making the first category of products will be your dream companies. You would want to design, make and sell products that customers love and buy again and again. This will ensure sustained growth and great returns for your company.

But, picking such products or companies is not easy. Is there a formula that guarantees product success?

"[Warren] Buffett buys companies with products that fill the basic needs of society, appeal to human emotions and evoke highly favourable images", says Author Nikki Ross, providing a few examples from some of Warren's investments: Gillette (fills a basic need, associated with grooming), See's candy (satisfies chocolate craving), Coca-Cola (quenches thirst).

Basic needs and emotional needs might be different for different people. But, we can look at the majority and arrive at the set of needs that they typically want to be satisfied. Then we can look at the brands that have got highly favourable images to satisfy those needs. For example, there may be hundreds of candies, but what are the few brands that come to people's minds when they think of their need for candy? This line of thinking provides the clue into those products and brands that have long term potential.

What if a great basic or emotional need exists, but there is no single brand that has captured people's minds in that area?

That's great news. We have a wonderful opportunity to build a product and a brand to fill that void!

We can use Warren's product-company-selection mechanism to also enhance our communication. If we have an idea and we want people to see it favourably, we can tie it to one of their basic or emotional needs and ensure that our idea satisfies those needs. Once this is established, they will favourably look at our idea and we can seize that moment to establish its benefits further!

☑ ***The Warren Lesson: Look for solutions that fill a basic or emotional need of society.***

38

Every Employee Contributes to the Success (or Failure)

The success of a company is usually linked to its chairman or CEO. At best, we might give credit to the next level of leaders who report to this top boss. Anyone below their level is considered part of the organisation, but not directly responsible for its success.

In fact, the same rule is followed when crediting people for the failure of a company. Top leaders are blamed when the company doesn't perform well. In the case of extreme flop shows, they may even lose their job.

Warren Buffett reminds us that the success or failure of a company is rarely a function of a few individuals. He feels every activity done by an employee (at any level) can strengthen or weaken that company.

For example, Warren wants us to think about the sales clerk behind the counter of a candy shop. When a customer walks in to buy some sweets, he or she may either smile and give a great experience to this customer or speak to them angrily and act as if they don't care whether the customer buys sweets or not. Depending on this clerk's behaviour on that day, the customer leaves the shop in a happy or angry mood. This reflects in the customer's feelings about the shop or the brand itself.

We may think of this as a single transaction that has no impact on the overall scheme of things. But, when we add thousands of such transactions performed by hundreds of staff members with thousands of customers, the impact adds up. In addition, the customers can also tell their friends and relatives about their experience. A positive word of mouth can help the company progress and a negative word of mouth can destroy it.

Hence, people working at every level of an organisation must understand the importance of doing the right things. In addition, their leaders and management team should also understand their importance, train them, respect them and treat them fairly. Such a company will grow fast as people give their best.

☑ **The Warren Lesson:** ***Every activity done by employees at all levels can strengthen or weaken a company. Hence, set the right message to employees, treat them well so that they can treat your customers well and the company can grow.***

39
Addressing Self-Doubt

Every year, the world is producing thousands of talented individuals. They start their career with limited experience, talent, tremendous hope and ability to work hard. As they progress, they gain experience and skills which help in their further growth.

However, this journey is not always smooth. They face roadblocks in their path now and then which they need to fight against. Many times these roadblocks are placed by other people or market situations. But, sometimes, they are placed by these individuals themselves.

A talented person won't put a roadblock for his/her own success knowingly. Some of the habits they had earlier or acquired during their work-life are responsible for this. One best example is self-doubt.

"I've never had any self-doubt", says Warren Buffett. "I've never been discouraged."

This may not surprise us because we know who Warren is today. But, his statement talks about his entire career which spans many decades. He was not the best investor in the world on the very first day of his career. He faced many hurdles and worked hard to win against them and reached the pinnacle of success. Even during those hard days, he didn't have self-doubt.

Not having self-doubt benefits someone in two ways: it doesn't pull them back, instead, it pushes them forward. So, the impact is 2x when compared to someone else with similar talents, but has self-doubt. Not being discouraged about things not going as per our plan and not blaming ourselves for the same are important mindsets that give us the enthusiasm to face the world and think of the next step. They tell us that the current state or the results of our earlier action don't define us and with a different approach, we will be able to produce a different result.

In addition to spotting and addressing our self-doubt, we should also be watchful of this habit in others. Many times, people move ahead and succeed because of the trust others show in them even when they doubt themselves. If we can play that role to others and encourage them to move forward, someone else will do the same to us when we need it the most.

☑ ***The Warren Lesson: Don't have self-doubt; don't feel discouraged; act with confidence.***

40
Meeting Obligations

Let us say there are two ways to run your business. The first way is to run it in a cautious way that allows you to get decent profits on a continuous basis, even when the conditions are adverse. The second way allows you to get great profits under normal conditions. But, if the conditions are bad, it may produce poor profits (or even losses). Which one will you select?

People who are comfortable in taking risks are likely to select the second way after doing some analysis. They would argue that the results will match the risk taken. When things go our way, we will make a lot of money, which will balance the poor performance during bad weather.

Warren Buffett says that he will select the first way in these circumstances because 'we do not wish it to be only likely that we can meet our obligations; we wish that to be certain.'

This means if a business runs for many years and has obligations to take care of, Warren's first priority as its leader is to ensure that those obligations can be met with certainty, even when things go wrong. To ensure this happens, he is okay to compromise on some additional profit which might be the prize for risk-taking.

"We adhere to policies that will allow us to achieve acceptable long-term results under extraordinarily adverse conditions, rather than optimal results under a normal range of conditions", says Warren. Notice that he doesn't talk about the percentage of times normal conditions occur because that calculation will simply tease the leader to think of the Risk Vs Rewards balance. Such a thought process will make it likely that in some years their business won't be able to meet its obligations. Warren feels it is not a worthy risk to take.

These obligations may differ from company to company. But, all of them have some obligation or other which they must meet on a consistent basis. For example, providing the best products or services to our customers, extending great support experience to them, bringing value to our stockholders, creating opportunities for our society, paying back loans, being a responsible corporate citizen and many others. When you keep these obligations as your priority, then 'acceptable results even under adverse conditions' looks better than 'optimal results only under normal conditions'.

Similar obligations exist for individuals too. They drive each one of our decisions. Meeting our obligations consistently makes others trust and respect us and improves our business and personal relationships.

☑ **The Warren Lesson:** ***Meet your obligations with certainty; That's an important priority for everyone.***

41

Short Read, Long Read

A few years back, one of my favourite newsletters introduced an interesting new feature: before beginning every article, they started stating the typical time it takes to read that particular article. For example, a short article might start with "Reading time: 2 minutes", while a long read might start with "Reading time: 12 minutes". Readers can look at this data and decide whether they want to invest this time or not, even before they start reading it.

Soon, many other publications such as websites, blogs and newsletters started announcing the reading time ahead of their articles. Readers expressed their pleasant surprise and many others followed this trend. In fact, Readers understood the value of this data in their decision making or article selection process so much so that they started mentally calculating the reading time even on those articles which didn't publish them explicitly.

Similarly, some people have the habit of announcing the time before starting a discussion. For example, they might ask, "I need to discuss something with you which might take 10 minutes. Are you available now?" This helps the other person decide whether they want to start that discussion at that time or not.

Warren Buffett advises us to think in a similar manner before starting any task. "Understand the natural time horizon of the task you are set out to do. If you can't stand that time, do not do it."

For example, if someone wants to be an entrepreneur, he/she should be prepared for many months, if not years, of hard work. That's the typical time horizon of that task. If this understanding is not there and someone enters there expecting a quick win, they will be disappointed.

But, some entrepreneurs win quickly. Don't they?

Yes. But, are there rules or exceptions? We should always look at a larger sample set and understand what is the typical time it takes for a certain task. Then we should be mentally prepared to give that effort and not give up in between. If we can't, it is better we don't enter there at all. We should find another task that matches with our time expectations and that is likely to be a better fit for us.

☑ **The Warren Lesson:** ***Understand the time each task takes; if you can't invest that time, don't start that task.***

42

Necessary Prudence

You are walking on a busy road. Many people are walking along with you or coming in the opposite direction. All of you are walking at a normal, gentle pace and it looks like a usual day.

Suddenly, a bell rings and everyone (except you, of course) go wild. They start moving in unpredictable patterns in whichever direction they think of. Some of them even run and jump. The road has become a dangerous place.

In such a situation, what will you do? Remember that you are still not going wild and can think and decide!

When everyone around us is acting in a strange way, we needn't (and shouldn't) join them. In fact, that's the time we should be extremely careful because irrespective of what we do, someone else can cause damage to us. So, we should act in such a way that we protect ourselves and others, if possible.

A similar responsible thought process should come to our mind whenever we see trends around us. If the majority of the people act in a certain manner, that doesn't mean they are right. In fact, if those people are acting without thinking, it is better we break the chain and think before we act. This might help us and others too, who might look at our behaviour and understand that there is a different way to do things and they don't have to follow the majority all the time.

'The less the prudence with which others conduct their affairs, the greater the prudence with which we must conduct our own', says Warren Buffett. This means, when others are not being sensible or careful and taking unnecessary risks, we should pause and watch. We should be extremely careful and trust data and our analysis before proceeding.

On another occasion, he conveyed a similar message using a casino analogy, "You are dealing with a lot of silly people in the marketplace. It's like a great big casino and everyone else is boozing. If you can stick to Pepsi, you should be OK."

Being prudent is always a great skill to master. However, Warren's comments ask us to also observe whether others around us, especially our industry peers, are being prudent or not. When the majority of them are being less prudent, we should bear the responsibility and act with extreme caution, educating everyone about the benefits of such a thought process. It helps us stay on the right course while helping others.

☑ **The Warren Lesson:** ***If others are not prudent, we should be more prudent in our actions.***

43

A Successful Day

What is the definition of a successful day?

Some people tie the success of a day with the tasks completed or the goals achieved during the day. For example, they might have closed a large sales deal or written a fantastic program to solve a major customer problem. These would make them feel very happy and proud when they go to sleep that night.

However, there is a flip side to this thought process. If you consider achievements as the mandatory requirement for a day to be successful, a lack of achievements or the presence of a mistake will immediately make it a "day of failure". Such a black and white approach can put tremendous pressure on us as we will be seeking achievements every day, becoming more and more anxious if we can't find something. If everyone thinks like this, the work environment can become a continuous race where only a few can win on any given day.

Warren Buffett gives us a different yardstick to measure a successful day: being smarter at the end of the day than at the beginning of the day. If every day can be like this, we will grow in any field.

Compared to the race to achieve things continuously, this is a refreshing change and gives us a learning mindset. We may start with no knowledge or limited knowledge and follow this process every day to become a little bit smarter and all those add up to give us big gains.

For example, an employee or a manager or an entrepreneur does various activities throughout the day, meets people, gets feedback, reads articles, watches training videos and so on. If he/she constantly looks for learning opportunities in all these interactions, every day will add something or other to his/her skillset. Even a complex topic can be learnt bit by bit by following such an approach.

This is where habits become very important. If we can form a habit of continuously learning things and connecting the dots, we can learn anything and everything and stay ahead of others without participating in a daily race. We will have more happy and successful days and that will contribute to our mental health as well.

☑ **The Warren Lesson:** ***Become smarter at the end of the day than at the beginning of the day.***

44

The Win-Win Deal

Every financial transaction has two parts: a credit and a debit. A credit entry represents a transfer of value from an account and a debit entry represents a transfer of value to an account. This means each transaction transfers value from a credited account to a debited account.

In common terms, this means that every transaction involves someone losing value and someone else gaining value. For example, if you pay $10 to a shopkeeper, your account loses $10 and the shopkeeper's account gains $10.

We can see such transfers of value in various real-life scenarios as well. For example, when someone joins a company, they agree to transfer a value (their experience and expertise) to the company they are joining. In return, the company agrees to transfer a value (their salary and other benefits) to them.

Even when two companies or individuals are discussing a possible deal, the question of transfer of value applies. Both parties ask the important question, "What's in it for me?", in other words, "What will you (the other party) transfer to me?" If both parties can answer this question satisfactorily, there is a balance and they agree on a deal. Else, one of the parties may walk away from the deal because it is one-sided.

"Try to come up with deals that are good for both sides", says Warren Buffett. "Both sides should walk away thinking they won."

This means Party A should give something that Party B needs and vice versa. This makes both of them feel good about the transfer of value and a deal is signed.

Even individuals can use this advice from Warren effectively. When we need something from others, we can try to create this balance by offering a transfer of something of equal value immediately or in the near future. This makes it likely that they agree to give us what we need now. A similar question can be asked when others need something from us, making sure that the deal is good for both us and them.

☑ **The Warren Lesson:** ***Deals should be good for both sides.***

45

Value of Hard Work

When someone wants to write a book, he/she starts by doing deep research on the topic. They may read hundreds of thousands of pages of written material, meet experts in that domain or those who have first-hand experience working with the subject, analyse the available data and related research to connect the dots so that they can perfect their message, and take extensive notes. All these need to be done even before the first word can be written.

Many months or years later, someone might pick this book from a shelf and read it casually. They may not even realise that the author went through all these hardships to get this work released. But, it remains a fact and will be the guiding principle for others who may want to write books in the future. There are no shortcuts to hard work.

This is not restricted to books and authors. Every field has its own version of hard work necessary to produce something meaningful. This is especially true for those who are entering those fields as freshers; they may have to consume a lot of information before they can use all that knowledge to make the right decisions.

When Warren Buffett was getting introduced to the world of share market and stocks, he realised that no one is going to tell him the right thing to buy. In fact, such a piece of knowledge was not readily available anywhere. Hence, he figured out that he needs to go where the raw data is and start processing it however large it might be.

Warren says that during this time he was reading bulky manuals running hundreds of pages. He was reading them to find out more details about the potential items he could buy and used those details to make those decisions. This is how he spotted his early opportunities.

When we face large challenges, the sheer volume of work might overwhelm us. During those difficult times, we need to remember that if we work hard enough, we will find something of value. It may be searching for a needle in a haystack, but that's the only way we can progress and looking at the volume and getting surprised is not going to take us anywhere. Get started and get going, you will find your way.

☑ **The Warren Lesson:** ***Work hard, find your path.***

46

The Right Seed

Which one is more important: the destination or the path taken to reach there?

For example, a student scoring top marks and a sales representative winning a big deal have achieved great feats. But, if they used unfair means such as copying or bribing to get there, suddenly their achievements look flat. Even if no one knows the wrong methods employed by the student or the sales representative, it is against the universal laws.

Integrity is an essential element in any individual or organisation. Warren Buffett explains it beautifully, "Don't cut corners. You won't like it when you look back."

This reminds us of the proverbial, "answering the person in the mirror". He/she always knows that we have cut a corner and won't let us forget that. The world may praise us for our achievements, but this thought or knowledge that we have taken the wrong route to get there will continuously make us feel bad which won't be worth the effort.

In today's competitive world, success is respected and sometimes, means to achieve the same are ignored. Students are encouraged by others, even by some teachers and parents, to take shortcuts when they see them so that they can achieve greater things faster. Even if they feel bad about it, they are shown examples of others taking similar shortcuts and messages such as 'in the larger scheme of things, these shortcuts are nothing' try to comfort them.

If someone goes against this advice and firmly refuses to take a shortcut, they are immediately labelled as impractical. Slowly and steadily, society seems to take a view that winning matters, not the methods. We are trying to normalise wrong-doings as long as the result is favourable.

Mahatma Gandhi calls means as seeds and ends (results) as trees. Just like there is a strong connection between seeds and the trees that come out of them, means are linked to the end. As a poisonous seed will only give a poisonous tree, you can't achieve a good win with bad means. We need to remember this always, especially when faced with tough situations that present opportunities to take a shortcut. They are the times we should firmly say "No". This is not because we are afraid of someone finding it or putting us in jail, but because it is the right thing to do.

☑ ***The Warren Lesson: Don't cut corners. You won't like it when you look back.***

47

Talk and Action

"Talk is cheap", they say. This means anyone can lecture about the great things they are going to do or the wonderful principles they are going to follow. But, it is harder to put them into action. Until this is done, there is no value to all the things you say.

For example, a businessperson may say, "I will never cheat my customers or the government and I will always go by the rulebooks, even if it results in a loss to me." This tall talk about integrity is true only if he/she follows it in every situation.

What will happen if one doesn't really follow what he/she says?

The world is listening and watching. It attaches limited value to things people say, but tremendous value to things people do. If someone says something and does something else, it immediately results in a loss of reputation. On the flip side, those whose words and actions are in line get great respect.

This is especially true for parents. If they advise their children to do certain things and they themselves don't follow them, their children will never respect or follow them in this aspect. When they stop advising and start living the life they want their children to adapt, immediately they see their children following them, without the need for a single word of advice.

"It is not what you say, but what you do", says Warren Buffett. Instead of wasting words in describing the right behaviour, one can start following it or doing it, which is easier for others to follow. This applies not just to kids, but to everyone.

For example, if managers want their staff to prepare reports in a certain way, paying special attention to careful verification of facts and data, they can actually use the same method to write a few reports on their own. All their staff, especially those who want to improve and grow, will watch this and start following it. This is better than a lecture on how to write an effective report.

☑ ***The Warren Lesson: Instead of telling others what to do or how to do it, start doing it the right way and they will watch and follow.***

48

The Orangutan Effect

Warren Buffett wants to be remembered as a good teacher.

Yes, you read it right. When such a question was asked to him, he mentioned that he wants to be remembered not as a good investor, not as a good corporate leader, not as a good philanthropist, not as a good family person, but as a good teacher. While his other roles mentioned here are important and he respects his contributions in those roles, Warren wants to excel as a teacher so that he can help others grow and succeed.

Agreed, Warren is not a traditional teacher. He doesn't go to a university, lecture children or adults on various subjects, give them tests, correct their test papers or grade them. But, he has met hundreds of students from various educational institutes and taught them his life lessons. Hundreds of thousands of people have attended his sessions, read his articles and letters and learnt the art of investing and other topics. From this perspective, he is a great teacher.

Warren says that in addition to the benefits his students get from him, he too gets benefited from teaching. "Like writing, [Teaching has] helped me develop and clarify my own thoughts."

In other words, when we agree to teach something to others, we need to gather our thoughts, fine-tune them, identify and fill the gaps, read the counterarguments, analyse them well to understand the overall picture. All these add clarity and we understand the topic better even before we start teaching.

Warren's partner Charlie calls this the Orangutan Effect. Let us assume you are sitting with an Orangutan and trying to teach it some complex science lesson. The Orangutan may not learn anything from your teaching. But, your act of teaching it something will make you understand that topic better.

That's why we should eagerly grab any opportunity to teach any topic to anyone. While it might benefit others, it will definitely benefit us by giving more clarity on that topic. If we keep doing it, our thinking improves, the way we present facts improves and we become better communicators.

☑ **The Warren Lesson: *Teach Others; It will help you too.***

49

Good Decisions and Bad Decisions

Life gives us numerous opportunities for decision making every day. We keep making small, medium and large decisions on a regular basis which take us on different paths. This means that taking right decisions on a consistent basis can set us up for success.

Hence, decision-making skills are seen as a strength for any leader. They are trained to identify various options, weigh their pros and cons, analyse them and make a decision objectively. Some leaders even maintain a decision journal that records all the situations, their context, information considered, decision made, its eventual result and retrospective feedback on whether the decision was right or wrong. A regular review of this journal can help them make better decisions by using the power of experience.

There are many leaders who are expert decision-makers. But, even they can't claim all their decisions were right. It is a continuous learning process and their skills improve over time.

While we can feel happy about our good decisions, Warren Buffett advises us to give a careful look at our poor decisions regularly. "Knowing your poor decisions and knowing why they were poor is part of good decision-making."

For example, let us say you are responsible for deciding which products need to be stocked in your company warehouse and their respective quantities. A new product has emerged in the market and its manufacturer asks you to stock it in a good quantity so that you can fulfil the customer demand. But, you feel it is not mature enough to deserve a place in your expensive warehouse space. So, you decide not to stock it for the current month and make a mental note to relook at this product next month.

But, during that month, the product becomes a big hit among consumers and stores are asking for it in huge numbers. Unfortunately, you don't have the stock and it results in a big opportunity loss for your organisation.

Agreed, this is a bad decision. But, it won't make you a bad decision-maker. In the same month, you might have made 99 other good decisions that resulted in millions of dollars of additional revenue for your company. However, those 99 decisions can't teach you lessons that this 1 decision can. By carefully analysing it and by asking tough questions such as "why did I feel this product won't have high demand?", "what other information I could've reviewed before arriving at a conclusion like this?" etc. you can learn a lot and avoid a similar mistake in future.

Hence, when it comes to teaching us lessons, bad decisions are our best pals, including the bad decisions of others.

☑ **The Warren Lesson:** ***Look at your bad decisions; learn from them; it helps you make good decisions.***

50

The "Because" Test

Very often, people buy stocks because of inputs from others. These might be their neighbours or colleagues or relatives or friends, who may not even be stock market experts. But still, people listen and respect their inputs mainly because many of them lack the ability to do their own analysis about a company. Hence, listening to others and hoping for the best looks like the right thing to do.

Warren Buffett argues that buying a part of a business is a serious decision and one should do it only after careful analysis. He encourages people to take a piece of paper and write a statement like this: "I am buying the stocks of XYZ company at this price because….."

Imagine you are writing a similar statement for your grocery purchases. It is very easy to write it because we know why we are buying milk or fruit juice at a certain price. The same logic should apply to stocks as well and "my friend asked me to buy" can't be that reason.

Even if we don't invest in stocks, Warren's advice can still be used because we do various things on a regular basis and not all of them are based on a clear thinking process. Taking a minute to form a sentence such as "I am doing X because...", will help us ensure that we have a strong reason for doing those things. This can make us avoid unreasonable activities.

For example, let us say you are planning a meeting for 1 hour and inviting four people. You can take a piece of paper (or open a text file on your computer) and answer questions such as these: Do we really need this meeting? Can't this be resolved in an Email or a phone call? Why 1 hour? Can't this be discussed in 30 minutes? What about 15 minutes? Why do you need these four people in the meeting? Are they the right people? Are you missing anyone? Can it be done with less number of people? Why should this meeting happen this week? Can't it be moved to next week? What decisions do you expect to take in this meeting? What if this meeting is postponed for a month?

The "because" word in Warren Buffett's statement looks small. But, it opens a big set of questions and answering them is not easy. However, if we learn to answer them for everything we do and pass the "Because" Test, we are more likely to focus on the right things and drop the weak, ambiguous things.

☑ **The Warren Lesson:** ***Why are you doing this? List down your reasons; make sure they are strong reasons.***

51

Average Office, Amazing Portfolio!

Major league games get great media attention. People watch them regularly and follow their favourite teams and players. From stadium ticket sales to sponsorships to live telecast fees, these events bring a lot of money to the respective leagues.

Compared to these, Minor league games are not very popular. But, you still see the same passion, if not more, in the players. Why?

The first reason is that they love the game and want to play it well no matter whether it is a major league or minor league. In fact, a good player will show his/her skills even if it is a practice game not watched by anyone.

But, there is a second reason which makes minor league games interesting: they help junior players build a record of achievement. This acts as proof of their skills and consistency and can become their entry ticket for the major league selection.

Similar examples can be found in other fields also. A programmer can join an online coding challenge and build a repository of great works. Later, when he/she attends an interview, this repository can be used as proof of all the good work they have done in their field.

"I operated out of a small set-up for years", says Warren Buffett. "It was not set up to impress people. My numbers impressed people and that's how money came in. If you are a new person, try to get an auditable record of your achievement."

When we start operating in a field, we won't need a flashy office or a fancy website. Many freelancers start with their own home office and a free email address. However, they invest in building a great portfolio, which Warren calls an auditable record of achievements, so that they can use this as the real set-up which impresses future clients.

For example, a designer might work out of a small desk in her kitchen. But, if she has 20 high-quality designs made for a variety of clients and requirements, it can be used as the basis for inviting future work from her clients and prospects. The world will respect talent and we need to make sure we collect the proof of our talent in one place and present it right.

☑ **The Warren Lesson:** ***Build an auditable record of your achievements.***

52

Lunch with Warren

In 2007, Value Investor Mohnish Pabrai paid $650,000 for an opportunity to have lunch with Warren Buffett and Charlie Munger. The proceeds went to charity and Mohnish had a rare opportunity to discuss with and learn from these great investors.

When Mohnish spoke to author Morgan Housel about his lunch with Warren, he told that Warren put him at ease, making him think he is having lunch with his grandfather. This is a great gesture. But, Warren didn't stop there. He went ahead and gave a wonderful experience to Mohnish by answering his questions in a manner that gave him tremendous learning. Why?

Mohnish feels this is because Warren understood that this lunch was very important to the other person at the table. They have paid a huge sum of money not for the food items that are offered, but for the opportunity to speak to him personally. Agreed, the money goes to a good cause. But still, they will expect to get some value out of lunch with Warren. Hence,

Warren wanted to ensure that the guest doesn't feel disappointed about the conversation.

This incident not only demonstrates Warren's humility but also shows his great skill in seeing every interaction from the other person's view as well. Being a celebrity, he may have many items on his calendar, but still, he didn't treat this lunch as a usual transaction. He ensured providing the best value to the other party.

As our daily calendars are full of meetings and discussions, we tend to move from one conversation to another with minimal preparation and try to manage depending on the situation. While this may be seen as a smart hack, it doesn't do justice to other participants in the meeting for whom it may be a very important meeting and they may expect us to be there with deserving preparation. When we see meetings from this perspective, we won't see our calendars as a collection of 30-minute slots to be used for all sorts of meetings. We will learn to respect other participants and spend time on our preparation, we will be fully present (instead of "multitasking" on an e-mail or Document), we will listen carefully, ask the right questions, provide value in our responses and ensure the other participants have a great experience.

But, what if we are very busy and don't have the time to prepare well or to be present fully?

In that case, we should be upfront in asking for more time, stating the reason for the same. It is better to be well prepared and fully present than provide a less than perfect experience to other participants. They deserve better.

☑ **The Warren Lesson:** ***Give the best value and best experience to the other person at the table.***

53

Difficult Problems don't Need Difficult Solutions

Once upon a time, a soap company had a big problem: some of their soap boxes were empty which frustrated their customers. They felt cheated and complained loudly, which hurt the brand's reputation.

Hence, engineers working in that soap company gathered for a discussion, "how can we find those empty boxes and remove them before they reach stores?"

Within the next 30 minutes, the whiteboard in the meeting room was filled with diagrams. More than twenty solutions were captured. They involved electronic scanners, accurate weighing machines, robots and artificial intelligence software.

At that time, a junior staff member asked casually. "Instead of all these complex solutions, why not install a large fan in the conveyor belt which sends our soapboxes to the outside world?

If a box is empty, it will be removed from the conveyor belt by the wind from the fan."

This imaginary story teaches us a valuable lesson: complex problems don't need complex solutions. Sometimes, even simple things can help us resolve complex issues. As Warren Buffett says, "You are awarded no points in business endeavours for the degree of difficulty."

That doesn't mean we will always get a simple solution to any problem. We should expect a mix of solutions. Some of those solutions could be so simple and easy that anybody can understand and even implement them. However, a few other solutions will be in a medium or large complexity/difficult level which might need a deeper understanding of the context and technologies before we can move towards a solution. All these solutions need to be analysed before the best one is selected. Sometimes, the best solution could even be a combination of two or more solutions of various complexity levels.

While doing this solution analysis, some of us have a bias towards complex solutions (and a negative bias towards simple solutions). We somehow feel complex problems need complex solutions and hence look down on solutions that might be too simple. In reality, "degree of difficulty" or "complexity" is not an important part of such decision making. As long as the solution solves the problem well, it should be adapted. As every computer user might know, even the most complex problems can be solved by closing and reopening a window!

Hence, when we are analysing possible solutions to a problem, we need to remove the bias towards complex or difficult solutions and focus entirely on solving the problem. Hard work is good, but if some easy work solves the issue, who would say no to it?

☑ ***The Warren Lesson: There are no points in business endeavours for "degree of difficulty".***

54

The Need for Immediate Help

A friend calls you with an urgent request, "Hey Buddy, one of my business decisions flopped and I need to do some damage control. Can you help me with this?"

"Sure, I will be happy to do that", you reply enthusiastically. "Let us meet over a cup of coffee and discuss it. I am sure we can sort the problem out and you will be back to normalcy soon."

Within a few hours, you both meet in a cafe and your friend explains his decision and its current state. He proposes the next steps he has identified and asks for your inputs and help.

Now, your friend has acknowledged his error and made it clear that he is expecting your views and support on the next step. Instead of that, if you start with strong criticism on why he shouldn't have taken that business decision in the first place, how will he feel?

Unfortunately, many of us make this mistake when working with people who are in desperate need of support. We like pointing out their mistakes (which they might have realised by now) instead of focusing on the next steps. This puts them in a disadvantaged position to correct the error which has happened.

Notice that no one is denying their error. A good friend or guide will point it to them and help them avoid similar mistakes in future. However, there is a time and place for it. When there is damage control to be done to ensure normalcy, discussing the past is not the optimal use of our time.

Warren Buffett uses the example of someone ill to describe this process. At that time, the expectation is not to criticise them for not following healthy habits or for not testing earlier. We should only look ahead to the treatment required to cure them.

Even when thinking in that direction, Warren advises us not to worry or argue too much about the accurate treatment. Instead, we should focus on what needs to be done immediately with the best information and resources in our hands. As we start this first aid, slowly more data emerges and we can move towards the right solution.

After the issue is resolved and the person in front of you can smile comfortably, you can gently remind them about some of their earlier wrong choices and ensure that they have learnt their lesson. They are more likely to listen to you now because they are not anxious about the issue and can understand and take action with a clear mind.

☑ **The Warren Lesson:** ***When someone has a problem, instead of criticising them or worrying about the right solution, get to the best action according to what you know at that time.***

55

Earning and Spending

Every person on earth does a balancing act of income and expenses almost daily. They do some work or run a business and earn money which acts as their money input. On the flip side, they have bills to pay, items to buy and services to use which cost money. These act as their money output. Depending on which one is higher and by what amount, they may save some money or they may have to borrow some money from others.

When people don't realise the importance and value of saving, they tend to spend whatever they earn and live paycheck to paycheck. Even if their salary or income increases, they tend to increase their spending and still manage to live paycheck to paycheck. The increased income is seen as a licence to spend more and enjoy more.

Warren Buffett encourages people to spend only when necessary, even when they have a lot of money. This can be done by carefully analysing our spending, ensuring that each expense is justified for both its purpose (is this required?) and the amount (is this the right amount to spend?).

We can see many examples of this habit in Warren's life itself. While other rich people live in large mansions with fancy facilities, he is famous for living in the same house for decades. His children attended normal schools attended by other kids in the neighbourhood. Just because Warren had money, he didn't throw it on unnecessary stuff.

Spending wisely reduces our expenses and allows us to save more. These savings can then be invested in something right, like what Warren did. In addition, it also provides us with a useful life skill: being conscious about where our money goes. Those who don't have this skill will constantly complain about losing everything they earn and won't even realise that they are the prime reasons for this issue. Even if their income doubles or triples, they will still have the same problem because they automatically increase their expenses in the same ratio. On the other hand, those who spend wisely will watch their expenses and will be able to adjust them as per the need.

☑ **The Warren Lesson:** ***Spend Wisely.***

56

Facing Pain

A driver in a new city misses spotting a red light at a traffic signal. Only after jumping the signal does he realise his mistake and say, “Oops! I am in trouble.”

He is a good citizen and doesn’t want to run away from his mistake. So, he pulls over to the side of the road and waits for someone to come and give him a ticket. He mentally prepares himself to seek an apology and pay the necessary fine.

But, surprisingly, nothing of that sort happens. Even after many minutes of waiting, no one comes over and gives him a ticket. So, he moves away from the place, full of guilt.

A few days later, he faces a similar situation. Once again, no one noticed and no one blamed him for the error. Next month, the same pattern repeats once again and he gets away from yet another traffic violation ticket.

Now, imagine what impact this will have on that driver’s mindset towards respecting traffic rules. He has made three mistakes already and got away from them. So, he is likely to press his luck more and make more such mistakes. On the contrary, if he was punished for his first offence itself, he would've become extra careful in his driving and would've followed all traffic rules dutifully.

Warren Buffett reminds us that such behavioural patterns can be observed even in our offices. When we make a stupid decision and no one notices or tells us that we could've done something better, we tend to underestimate the effect of such stupid decisions. Instead, if we feel some pain (of hearing tough feedback or even a few harsh words from our superior) immediately after the stupid decision, we are likely to use it as a lesson to improve our future decisions.

Hence, our attitude about feedback should change dramatically: hearing 'you are doing good' from everyone all the time is not necessarily good news and hearing 'you did something really stupid' is not necessarily bad news. In fact, the pain we feel ourselves, or the pain which is given by others to us for doing something wrong acts as an effective guide in guiding our future decisions in the right way.

☑ **The Warren Lesson:** ***When you make a bad decision, face the tough feedback, feel the pain and use it to improve your future decisions.***

57

Success, Guaranteed!

A company can win a customer's business in many ways: providing a high-quality product or service, keeping their price competitive, offering world-class support, advertising in the right channels, reaching out to the customer in their own spaces, being environmentally responsible and so on. These are great techniques and are likely to help the company succeed. But, there is another way that combines the power of all these and almost guarantees its success: deserving the customer's business.

GEICO, one of the major companies in Warren Buffett's empire, has a long history. It has served multiple generations of people and many things about this company have changed over time: leaders, managers, products, sales channels, support channels, marketing channels, advertising platforms, payment methods and so on. But, Warren states that its core goal has remained unchanged: saving Americans' substantial money on their purchase of auto insurance. By doing this, they deserve the customer's business and make it a very simple and straightforward choice for them. By focusing on this objective, GEICO grew its market share and became one of America's largest auto insurers.

When a product deserves the customer's business, its makers don't have to explicitly convince them about it. There won't be any need for fancy marketing literature listing down the product's features and benefits; comparison charts showing its superiority against competitors won't be necessary. Even if these materials exist, the customer will simply say, "I am already convinced because you deserve my business."

For many, this may look like an unbelievable, unachievable dream. But, it is possible. History is rich with examples of many companies building such products and customers welcoming them with open arms giving their unconditional loyalty. This magic happened because those companies focussed entirely on their customers. They understood their customers' needs, pain points, expectations and feelings and built something which takes care of these and becomes an automatic choice for customers.

This doesn't mean those companies neglected other factors in product/service development. They are important too; but addressing the customers' problems and giving them a satisfactory solution should be their core objective. When a product or a service is made with such care and love, it shows and customers will understand it readily!

☑ **The Warren Lesson:** ***Build something that deserves the customer's business.***

58

Heroes won't Let you Down

Who was your childhood hero (or heroine)? What about school days? College days? Early career? Now?

These heroes and role models may not be the same people. As we grow, our interests change, our definitions of success and achievement change, we start looking at nuances that we missed earlier and these changes help us look up to different people at different ages and it is quite normal.

Also, these heroes needn't be big achievers or people with special skills. They may be ordinary individuals whom we respect due to various reasons; they may be people whom we want to become because we admire certain great qualities in them.

"Having the right heroes will help you manage tough times in life", says Warren Buffett. "If you tell me who your heroes are, I can tell you what you will become to some extent."

Warren had some great heroes in his own life: his dad, his wife and his professor Benjamin Graham. He feels these terrific heroes never let him down throughout his life and that took him a long way, especially when facing tough times in life.

This is where obsessing over a few people we like becomes a strength. We may read books about them, hear stories from others, we may read their own works and understand how they think, we may even be lucky enough to speak to them and learn from them directly. All of these form a picture in our mind which acts as a guideline whenever we face issues. We don't have to compare ourselves with people around us, who may be good folks, but work-in-progress like us! A simple question like, "how will my hero face this situation? what will he/she do?" can help us think straight and arrive at a better decision. Even if that hero or role model lived a few centuries back, he/she is still able to guide us and help us become better people.

☑ **The Warren Lesson:** ***Having heroes helps you!***

59

Use the Available Interstate

Until a few decades back, libraries were the largest sources of knowledge. If someone wanted to know about a topic, he/she had to go to the local library and patiently go through many books on that subject. It took a lot of time, but there were no other better options.

Today, this problem is solved with the help of technology. A student can access all the books, videos and audios about almost any subject with a few clicks online. Reading every book, every chapter, every paragraph, every line won't be necessary as a quick search will give them the information they need. They can even directly reach out to experts in that field from all over the globe and clarify their doubts without leaving the comforts of their homes.

Now, if a modern student refuses to use all these facilities and insists that he/she would research using the good old library method only, will it be the right use of his/her time? If some materials are not available online, they can always use an older method. In all other situations, they should use the available new technologies so that the saved time can be used for some other useful purpose.

Warren Buffett uses the analogy of a country road and an interstate road to explain this difference. If our current location and the destination are connected using a modern interstate road, we wouldn't be using an old country road to reach the same destination. Using the modern road saves us time, energy and fuel.

However, all these savings are possible only if we are aware that such an interstate road exists. Else, we will still be using the old, inefficient road. Similarly, we should keep our eyes and ears open to understand the latest and modern developments in our field and equip ourselves with the right skills as necessary. This gives us the best chance to use those advancements and get things done in a faster, efficient manner.

For example, there may be an online forum where experts from our domain usually discuss interesting topics. If we are aware of the existence of such a forum, we can read those conversations regularly and improve our knowledge. In addition, if we have a question or a doubt, it can be posted there for a quick and detailed response. This will be more efficient than posting the same question on Facebook and hoping that some expert would notice that and answer our question. We will know the presence of such forums and other tools only if we keep ourselves updated about the latest happenings in our field.

☑ **The Warren Lesson:** ***Use the most efficient tool available to perform any activity.***

60

Focus on Positivity

Certain online and mobile apps allow us to capture our mood on a regular basis. You can do it daily or every few hours or even every hour. Idea is to capture how your mood changes over a period of time, analyse it and determine corrective actions, if any.

Let us say someone uses one such app for a few weeks to dutifully record all his/her emotions. Later, he/she looks at the dashboard to understand the trend or pattern. It gives him/her a shocking truth: you are feeling negative most of the time.

More than the shock, he/she is surprised because "I never considered myself as a negative person. Of course, I feel down now and then; but didn't realise that it is affecting me so much."

This situation might look simple or amusing to some. But, it needs to be understood and addressed before it becomes a larger issue. They should focus on understanding various reasons that can cause this problem and handle them with the help of a professional, if required.

For example, they may be holding grudges against others which they may not even remember, but they stay deep inside and make them feel negative whenever they see those other people or related triggers. Similarly, they may feel negative things and have negative thoughts about how things will happen, "What if this fails?", "What if that doesn't work?"

Sometimes people around them may have continuous negative thoughts and spread negativity to others. In those cases, even if someone is usually optimistic about life, these thoughts will come and bother them unknowingly.

Warren Buffett advises us not to keep grudges or negative feelings about any people. He also encourages thinking of positive things and working with positive people. While this looks like an old styled solution, he assures us that it works.

In many interviews and letters, Warren continuously talks about the people he works with and how great they are. Whether it is professional associates or personal friends, he likes to spend time with positive people and it keeps him energised.

This doesn't mean we shouldn't think of risks or take necessary steps to mitigate them. While doing so, we should remember that thinking of these risks and mitigations early puts us in a better position to complete the task at hand successfully. Having a healthy environment where the focus is on progress, growth and making things happen shifts the spotlight from the possible negativity and allows us to stay happy.

People generally give a lot of importance to physical health and staying fit. But, mental health doesn't get the attention it deserves. Feeling good and positive about work and life in general is a non-negotiable aspect we all deserve.

☑ **The Warren Lesson:** ***Avoid holding grudges or negative feelings; think positively; work with positive people.***

61
The Pricing Power

Pricing a product or service right is an important skill. It depends on various factors such as the raw materials used to manufacture the product, cost of producing each unit, profit margin and so on. After considering all these, the company makes a pricing decision and regularly reviews it to ensure they stay competitive while continuing to make money.

Hence, when a product's price is increased, it can't be attributed to the company's greed by default. Sometimes, greed or making more money can be the reason for such decisions. But they are rare cases and companies usually increase the price because other input parameters have changed. They normally resort to this as the last option and try to avoid it as much as possible. When it becomes inevitable, they go for it with an apologetic mindset, "Dear Customer, we tried to avoid this as much as we could. But, now we should increase our prices. We understand this is inconvenient for you. But, we have no other option. Please understand and cooperate. We value your business."

This message shows the humble attitude with which companies approach a price increase because customers' reactions to it can make or break a company. Sometimes, they accept the price increase and continue to be loyal to the company. Some other times, they reject the price increase and move to a competitor who offers something similar at a lesser price. Whether they continue to stick around or jump depends on various factors such as product quality, how important or necessary is its need, the quality of competitors, the gap between the new price and the competitors' price and the corresponding quality gap, if any. Customers think about all these before making their final call. If customers do that analysis and accept your price increase, it indicates that your company has something called "Pricing Power", which means, you have the power to determine the right price for your product, not others.

"The single most important decision in evaluating a business is pricing power", says Warren Buffett. "If you've got the power to raise prices without losing business to a competitor, you've got a very good business. If you have to say a prayer before raising the price, then you've got a terrible business."

We must remember that the decision always lies with the customer. But, we have many factors in our hand which can be used to control their decision: building a world-class product, making it rightly priced and increasing the price only when necessary, being so ahead of other competitors that customers won't even consider them as alternatives, creating a loyal fan following etc. These are the raw materials that give us the Pricing Power and the success.

This can apply to individuals as well. When someone interviewing for a job can show all the required skills, but can't command the right salary, it shows a lack of Pricing Power. They should do a self retrospect and understand what it takes for them to get the salary they deserve and fill those gaps. Being able to control their own price is an ultimate power that differentiates great companies/people from others.

☑ **The Warren Lesson:** ***Do you have the power to price your product right? If not, what can you do to acquire that power?***

62

The Game of Liked and Disliked Qualities

Sometimes, Warren Buffett plays an interesting life game with his audience: he asks them to take a sheet of paper, draw a vertical line and split it into two parts. Then, they should think about people they know and list down all the qualities they like in those people on the left side of the paper. They should repeat the same process for the qualities they dislike in those people and write them on the right side of the paper. Finally, he asks them to analyse both the lists and see if any patterns are emerging.

For example, on the left side, we may have qualities such as hard work, humility, eagerness to learn and so on. The right side may be filled with qualities such as anger, not being able to complete things on time, disrespect to others etc.

Warren's theory is that the qualities on the left side (those we like in others) are not difficult to get. It won't have items like scoring 99% in every exam or being able to run a 100 metre race in 9 seconds or being the most beautiful person in the office. The real things we like in others are qualities that are achievable to anyone and everyone if they want them and try sincerely.

Similarly, the qualities on the right side are not things people can't get rid of. They are not must-have qualities. If someone has those qualities and wants to remove them, they can do it with practice.

When we admire certain qualities in people and know that we can have them too, why not make an attempt? When we dislike certain qualities in people and know that we too can get rid of them, why not make an attempt? A combination of these will make us much better than where we are today and doing this continuously will help us mature, grow and become the best we can be.

☑ **The Warren Lesson:** ***Think about the qualities you like or dislike in others. Then, compare those qualities with what you have and don't have. Such an analysis helps you improve and grow.***

63

Compounding Value of Learning

Constantly educating ourselves is an important skill today. As the world around us moves and changes, new things evolve and we need to unlearn and relearn so that we can make use of the new opportunities that emerge. People who are rigid about their past learnings score less when compared to those who are flexible in their approach.

This means that education doesn't have a full stop. You can't throw away books after you graduate from school and college. In your work life or entrepreneurial life, no one may publish a syllabus and give you a set of reference books to read. Instead, you decide your subjects and lessons on your own, by careful observation of your field and the trends. Then you can use a combination of books, videos, podcasts, talking to experts, working on new domains etc. to learn. Every professional should set aside certain hours for their self or guided learning.

But, how to make the best use of this time? How to determine the right things to learn that provide us maximum value?

Warren Buffett recommends that we start learning early (at a young age) to ensure the knowledge has an opportunity to compound over a long period of time. Hence, we should invest in learning things that have long term value and have the potential to compound.

For example, let us say a person spends 200 hours learning a specific programming language or a business tool. They are able to make the best use of their learning and get some immediate benefits. But, two years later, this language or tool becomes obsolete. No one in the market uses it or the original company which made it shuts it down. In this case, they have to restart the learning process again by focusing on a newer language or tool which is the market's favourite at that time. As this process repeats every few years, there is hardly any opportunity for their learning to compound and give multifold benefits.

Instead, let us say the same person spent 150 hours learning the basics of programming, logical thinking, high-level design, low-level design, optimised performance, etc. and only 50 hours on the programming language-specific details. The first part of their learning is going to compound for decades as those basics don't change very often. They can simply relearn programming language-specific topics every few years and use the solid basic understanding as the basis for their growth.

Hence, continuous learning is important; continuous learning of things that can compound over time is smart.

☑ ***The Warren Lesson: Invest in education early; Learn skills that can compound over time.***

64

Win Some, Lose Some, then Win Some More

When kids play a game, every win makes them happy and every loss makes them unhappy. Depending on the age and maturity level of the kids, they may even start laughing or crying when they face these results.

Thankfully, adults who face similar successes and failures on a regular basis don't react like that. However, there is no denying that we feel happy when things go as planned and unhappy when they take a different direction. We may not express it, but the inner ups and downs are always there.

People in leadership roles face this problem almost every day. Whenever they think about a problem and make a decision to solve it, they do it with a lot of care and expect it to be the right one. But, only a certain percentage of their actions and decisions turn out to be right. This means, they face successes and failures all the time.

Win Some, Lose Some, then Win Some More

"If every decision is perfect, it won't be fun", says Warren Buffett. He uses the analogy of a golfer who manages to get every ball hit in the right place. It may make the player extremely happy. But will it be an interesting game? Viewers certainly won't enjoy it. Actually, after some time, the player himself/herself may not like it. A game is fun only if it has those ups, downs and dramatic turning points.

For example, think about the most interesting sports event you ever watched in person or on television. Chances are high that it won't be a game where your favourite team or player won every point. They would've faced failures here and there and pushed hard to succeed. Those successes are more satisfying to players as well as viewers because we all understand bad things happen and what we do to them differentiates average people from extraordinary people.

Hence, Warren feels failures or mistakes are part of the game and they shouldn't discourage us from moving on. Every error or wrong call teaches us something. Once the lesson is internalised, we should try to focus on the next steps. Later, when a similar situation emerges, this learning can be used. Hence, we shouldn't let failures discourage our progress. They actually make the game more interesting by giving us additional motivation to push for success.

☑ **The Warren Lesson:** ***If everything goes perfect, the game won't be fun. Enjoy the ups and downs and move on.***

65

My Luxury

How do you define Luxury?

For some, it is the number of houses one owns, the size of those houses, the number of workers attending to their needs, the number of cars, the number of foreign vacations, the ability to wear costly suits, send kids to foreign universities, donate to causes they believe in etc. A few others measure luxury with not having to work or not having to worry about how much money is there in their wallet or bank account.

While these are practical definitions of luxury, its dictionary definition goes like this: a state of great comfort or elegance, especially when involving great expense. Notice that the expense part comes later and the focus is entirely on comfort and elegance which may even be achieved at a lesser cost. This seems to suggest that we don't have to spend a lot to live a luxurious life.

My Luxury

Warren Buffett, one of the world's richest people, lives a simple life. He looks at others showing off their wealth and understands them. But, he feels it is not for him, "If it [Showing off wealth] makes them happy, it doesn't do anything for me."

Does this mean Warren doesn't live a luxurious life?

He does. Just that his definition of luxury is different. "I'm happy when I can spend every day doing things that I like to do. That's my luxury."

Of course, Warren is not against spending. He owns a private jet. Many of his companies and other companies where he has invested depend on people spending their money on various products and services. His letters to Berkshire Hathaway shareholders regularly request them to buy things from Berkshire Hathaway owned firms.

However, houses, jewellery, cars, private boats and hefty bank balances are only expressions or external indicators of wealth. If they make one happy, great. But, being able to do what one likes every day without any restrictions is an important result of being wealthy. If someone has all the money, things in the world and yet is forced to spend a certain number of hours in front of an office desk they don't like, they may not be living a luxurious life after all.

Another important lesson from Warren's quote is his emphasis on the "My" word. One person's definition of luxury may not match another person's definition and hence a blind copy of someone else's lifestyle is less likely to give us happiness. True happiness and the feeling of luxury which comes with it are unique to each individual and they should look for them within themselves.

☑ **The Warren Lesson:** ***Do what makes you happy; That's luxury.***

66

The Unsalaried Employee

Do you know Warren Buffett once worked for zero salary?

It was before his Berkshire Hathaway days. He was managing money from many individuals (and all of his own funds) through a series of partnerships. Not one, not two, more than 10 partnerships. He didn't even have a secretary to run them. He was writing all the cheques, picking the right investments, getting personal delivery of all shares and so on. For all this hard work, he was not paid a salary. Instead, he was compensated if his partners secured returns above a threshold of 6%.

But, in a particular year, if their returns fall below 6%, Warren needs to take care of that shortfall against his share of future profits. Thankfully, Warren managed to get a "better than 6%" return every year and didn't face any such situation.

However, the strange policy of "you get paid only when you earn a decent return for everyone" would've made Warren a better analyser because his regular income and returns from his own investments in those partnerships are directly linked to his performance. Probably, that's where he learnt important lessons in not losing money and selecting the right investments which provide consistent returns.

Another instance where Warren agreed to work for almost no salary was when he worked under Benjamin Graham, one of his heroes. He didn't do it to learn something new from Benjamin Graham; instead, he wanted to be inspired by the master on a regular basis.

Sometimes, especially in the early part of our careers, we may be locked in a job that pushes us to a corner. Irrespective of whether others forced us to take those options or we willingly took them, they needn't be totally negative or useless experiences. In fact, some high-pressure environments teach us lessons that happy paths can't. We need to look at each situation and see what we can get from them. These learnings will come in handy when the tough road ends and our smooth journey begins.

☑ **The Warren Lesson:** ***Even tough situations have takeaways; learn from them.***

67

I Don't Know!

When attending a job interview, one of the biggest fears in the minds of the job candidate is not knowing the answer to a question. They are hesitant to use the words "I don't know" because they can be seen as a direct reflection of their knowledge or talent. Hence, they conclude that the interviewers may reject them for not knowing an answer and wish for only those questions which they can answer comfortably.

Answering every question asked in an interview might be a great indication of someone's skills and knowledge. But, except for some rare, clearly defined topics, it is difficult, impractical and even impossible for someone to know all the answers. Even if someone manages to remember all the answers, it only proves that they have a great memory.

Practically speaking, even experts don't know all the answers. So, it is a wrong expectation in an interview setting.

You should prepare well and try to get all the answers right, but having it as the mandatory expectation is unreasonable.

Hence, experts recommend that interviewees should remove the fear of 'not knowing an answer' and they should be willing to admit that they don't know the answer to some of the questions. Trying to avoid this and giving some fake answers to those questions may be more dangerous than simply saying, "Sorry, I don't know." As long as you don't repeat this for every question, this won't be seen as a personal weakness and in most cases, the interviewer will simply smile understandingly and move on to the next question.

This fear of saying "I don't know" extends beyond interview settings. When we work in a company or face media interviews or answer audience questions in a public forum or even when a neighbour's kid asks us a question, we are hesitant to admit that we don't know the answer. We believe it will make us lose face in front of all those people.

Contrary to popular belief, saying "I don't know" to a question for which you don't know the answer actually enhances your reputation as you are being transparent and honest. If it is an important detail that you should've known, gently apologise, promise that you will get back to them with the answer and genuinely research, find out the answer and close the loop by conveying it to the person who asked the question. This is a much better approach that will benefit you and the other person.

"Tough questions are fine", says Warren Buffett. "If we [Warren and his partner Charlie Munger] know the answer, we will try and respond. If we don't know the answer, we will say we don't know it."

If Warren and Charlie, seen as great experts in their domain, face tough questions now and then and say "I don't know", we all should take it as a licence and use it in genuine cases. As long as it is followed up with a quest for learning, admitting that we don't know an answer is not a weakness, but a strength.

☑ ***The Warren Lesson: If you don't know the answer to a question, admit it.***

68

The Right Story

Bob Woodward, a famous journalist and author, became rich at a relatively young age. He once met Warren Buffett and asked for his advice on how to handle his money.

Warren used the terminologies from Bob's own field (journalism) to answer this question, "Assign yourself the right story, research, write and deliver it as per the timeline."

In a world full of stories, journalists can't write every story even if they want to. They need to look at the possible story leads, decide what makes them excited, assign it to themselves (or take assignments from senior journalists or editors) and start researching. Then they should read the right sources, speak to the right experts to get details about this story and perform fieldwork until they have all the required raw materials to write. Finally, they should write it and deliver it before the given time. This is a standard process in any newspaper or magazine.

Warren feels investing is just about assigning yourself the right story. If you want to invest in a particular asset class or in a particular company, you need to assign that story to yourself, do the required research, arrive at a decision and move on with the investment if it makes sense. Just like stories, there are too many investment possibilities and we need to pick the right story so that we make best use of our time.

Also, we need to understand that we are not capable of writing all the stories. There may be some topics for which Warren is not the right person to write. This is perfectly acceptable as long as there are other areas and topics which he can write about.

Warren's advice makes sense even in fields other than investing. Every task, every project, every program we take up, can be visualised as a story and we can go through to assign it to ourselves, research, write and deliver methodology. If the right stories are picked, we will be motivated to follow the remaining steps and over time, our repository of work will grow, resulting in our progress.

☑ **The Warren Lesson:** ***Assign yourself the right story and work on it.***

69

Financial Support from Customers

One of the many things you need to start a business is capital. Some people use their personal savings to start their business; a few others borrow money for this purpose; it is also a common practice to get financial support from friends, family and coworkers and give them a share of the business.

Warren Buffett points out that Insurance companies typically get financial support from their customers. That is, customers prepay an amount (premium) for their coverage and the Insurance company has the advantage of using this money for its business development. Of course, they have a commitment to pay the customer or their dependents if and when the covered risk occurs. But, in general, the money is available for immediate use.

Not all businesses can enjoy such advance payments or financial support from their customers. But, there are industries where such practices exist which can be a great idea for newbies willing to enter the world of business.

For example, Joe Mansueto, founder of MorningStar Inc., started a publishing business precisely because of this advice from Warren. As publishing companies collect subscription amounts from people in advance to provide their publications over a period of time, it acts as financial support coming directly from their customers. Joe mentions that this seemed a perfect option as he didn't have much capital when he started.

Another recent example is the advent of SaaS (Software as a Service) companies. These are built by passionate programmers who create a basic version, demonstrate it to the world, collect subscriptions from the customers and use it to build more features and grow. In fact, many of these companies provide a good discount for upfront annual payments instead of monthly payments so that they can have a better cash flow supported by loyal customers.

Getting financial support from the customers has the dual benefit of taking care of your capital needs to grow the business and giving you a longer commitment of business from them. When you know hundreds or thousands of people have agreed to use your product or service over a long period, there is no question of "who will use my creation?". We can be assured that people will use it and they have confirmed this by opening their wallets. This acts as a motivation to keep the bar high and build some wonderful solutions for them, which in turn can get us more financial support from the new customers they bring in. A perfect upward spiral! Hence, even if your business or industry doesn't seem to have a customer-funded innovation model, you can go out of your way to find creative ways to make it happen.

☑ **The Warren Lesson:** ***Can you get the financial support of your customers to grow your business?***

70

Great Author, But...

An author is invited to a conference to talk about the art of writing. He is thrilled and accepts the invite. He prepares well and delivers a speech rich with data and insights.

But, when the feedback came, his session scored the least. The audience didn't like it even though most of them are big fans of his writing. How is this possible?

When you are great in one field, that brings fame and following. Hence, even if you do something else in a related or unrelated field, people tend to notice. For example, if a famous actor sings a song, people want to listen to it because of the popularity he has already gained in another field. But, there is no guarantee that they will love the song or buy his future albums. It happens only when the actor is talented in both acting and singing.

Similarly, this author is great at expressing himself in words. But, when it comes to presenting them on stage, his public speaking skills are not as great as his writing skills and hence he is not able to make an impression. This is not a thing to be ashamed of because everyone can't be an expert in everything. As long as we understand where we are good and where we are average or below average, we will be able to set up our careers accordingly.

"We are all duds at one thing or another. For most of us, the list is long", says Warren Buffett. "The important point to recognise is that if you are Bobby Fischer, you must play only chess for money."

This learning extends beyond individual skills. When you want your organisation to diversify and enter a new product line or geography, you should do a careful analysis to understand whether we are as good as our current product line or geography in the new one too. If we realise that we are going to be duds there, either don't enter or enter with lower expectations and slowly build your skills to become better in the new area. Having this mindset avoids disappointments and helps us focus on the right things for success.

☑ **The Warren Lesson:** ***Understand what we are good at and do only that for money.***

71

Doing after Understanding

A friend of mine regularly invests in stocks. He doesn't understand the basics of the share market or does his own research. He doesn't even know much about most of the companies he invests in or the domains in which they operate. Instead, he follows some great experts who are good at analysing trends and giving recommendations and he simply goes by their advice. "My returns are great", he declares. "Much better than what I expected."

I feel happy for my friend and want him to be successful. Yet, I also remind him that his formula has a weakness: he does things without understanding them. He might have the backing of experts and trust them fully. But, if any of them makes a wrong judgement or purposefully gives a wrong recommendation that is favourable to them, my friend is going to suffer because he hasn't invested time in understanding what he is doing.

"When you start doing things that you don't understand or because they worked last week for somebody else, [it] doesn't work", warns Warren Buffett. He is a big advocate of individual research and taking investment decisions with full understanding.

However, what Warren says also applies in fields other than investment. If a company welcomes its new employees with, 'simply do what your seniors are doing' instruction, they are not setting up those young people for long term success. Instead, if seniors explain each task very well, with clear inputs on why they are done in a certain way, juniors understand what they are doing and are likely to become better at them. If they don't understand, they should be encouraged to ask questions until things are clear and they are not simply following someone's instructions. Even questions like "why are we not doing things some other way?" should be welcome because a new pair of eyes can spot some missed opportunities.

Similarly, whenever we are set to do anything new, we shouldn't narrow our focus to the usual questions of "What needs to be done?" and "How it needs to be done?" We should extend it by another important question, "Why is it done this way?" If the answer to this question is "I don't know" or "This is how we always did it", or "This worked for someone else", we should push back and analyse further until we understand why we are doing things in a certain way. Something that worked for someone else in another situation may not work for us because our conditions or even goals/targets may not be the same. Hence, a detailed analysis will give us clarity on whether it is likely to work or not and will guide us in the right direction, reducing the risk of failure. That's how we arrive at the unique solution which will work for our unique requirements.

☑ ***The Warren Lesson: Don't do things you don't understand just because they worked for others in some other situations.***

72

Fair or Wonderful?

Let us say you have a small amount of money in hand. You can use it and buy one of the following drinks:

1. A great drink which you love, which makes you feel happy and gives you energy for hours. It is normally worth $15 but is now available for $10.
2. A decent drink that is not bad, but not something you adore. It is normally worth $5 but is now available for $1.

When you go by pure calculations, the first drink is available at a 33.33% discount, while the second drink is a great bargain as it is available at an 80% discount. As the second drink's current price is much smaller than that of the first drink, you might be able to buy a higher quantity as well.

However, when we pick the drink, mathematical calculations are not the only things in our minds. We also look at the quality of the drink and what benefit it can bring to our body and mind.

With this context, you may give a higher weightage to the first drink which is not deeply discounted, but still, you feel it is a better choice.

When Warren Buffett started investing in companies, his strategy was to look for Cigar Butt Stocks, which means fair businesses available at wonderful prices. You pay a small amount to get a decent business and wait for it to grow a bit so that you can make some profit. This is exactly like picking a cigar butt thrown on the floor. It looks dirty, but it still has one puff left in it and you get it for free!

However, a cigar butt from the floor will only give you one puff. After that, you need to look for another cigar butt elsewhere.

Warren's partner Charlie Munger had a different idea: buy wonderful businesses at fair prices instead of fair businesses at wonderful prices. This means, paying a bit more (a fair price) but investing in a great business that is likely to grow big. This way even though the initial investment is (comparatively) high, the returns are expected to be much bigger and bring wealth. Warren adapted this strategy which helped both of them and their company.

We can use this lesson when we invest our money or time in any project: instead of focusing on things that have a low entry cost and light benefits, we can focus on things with a fair entry cost, but higher benefits. For example, if there is a business or technical skill that is easy to learn (less time investment), and the returns are small, is it really worth the effort? Instead, we can look beyond and find another skill which demands a higher time investment but is likely to get us much better returns.

☑ **The Warren Lesson:** ***Look for wonderful results at a fair cost, instead of fair results at a wonderful cost.***

73

Same Question, Fifth Time!

Recently, I attended a webinar as one of its speakers. As the audience doesn't know me personally, I prepared a short introduction (sort of a 2-minute elevator pitch) and presented it before presenting my topic. It went well and I felt the audience would've got a fair idea about me.

But, technology was not on my side on this occasion. The organisers of the webinar told me that they couldn't hear me properly and asked me to repeat the introduction for the benefit of everyone. I sighed and repeated the introduction.

While doing so, I noticed an interesting difference between my first and second introductions. Both were almost the same, I used the same words and similar sentences, facts didn't change. But, the second introduction didn't have the passion and energy of the first introduction. When I had to repeat my introduction, I suddenly lost interest and just did an average job.

The reason for this difference lies in human psychology which prefers to do new things. If we have already seen something or done something, seeing it or doing it again rarely brings us the same level of excitement and energy. We would prefer to do something else which is new and innovative.

However, our personal and professional life demands that we do certain things again and again, whether we like it or not. For example, when you are speaking to a new business associate for the first time, you need to talk about yourself and your program which you might have done 100 times earlier. Sometimes different people ask us the same question and we are forced to repeat the same answer. It is also possible that the same person asks the same question to us after a few days because he/she didn't pay attention to the answer the first time or simply forgot all about it. These instances make us frustrated and do a less than perfect job.

Journalist Anthony Bianco observes that Warren Buffett answers even the lamest questions with the same expansiveness and wit, even if he is hearing them for the fifth time. We can observe this if we watch four or five interviews with Warren where most of the questions (and his answers) tend to repeat. But, we won't spot any tiredness or irritation or lack of interest in Warren's voice or expressions. He will try to present the same answer with the same enthusiasm because he believes the answer truly.

There is another important reason too: it may be the fifth time he is hearing this question. But, for the person who is asking that question, it is new and they want to hear his answer in the best possible manner. They deserve it!

☑ **The Warren Lesson:** ***Even if you have to repeat yourself, be enthusiastic and do a good job every time.***

74

Compatible Partners

Having partners is a great way to get ahead with a complex task such as starting and running a business. This is because one person can't be an expert in every skill that is required to perform that complex task. Hence, if multiple people collaborate and bring different skills to the table, they can complement each other and run a successful show with each contributing in a different way.

For example, a few friends may become partners and start a magazine each contributing differently: writing, field research, interviewing, editing, proofreading, designing the pages, collecting advertisements, distribution, collecting subscriptions, handling foreign publishing rights and so on. Together they are able to bring the magazine successfully and share the returns.

However, such a partnership works only when those partners are compatible with each other. For example, if one of those partners joins this magazine expecting quick money, while the other partners have a long term business plan, he/she is likely to face disappointment and exit. Or, worst, he/she may try to influence others to change the business strategy which can result in the magazine losing its original vision.

Warren Buffett's suggestion to handle this problem is to find compatible partners by setting the ground rules and expectations clearly. This acts as a filter that keeps others (who are not compatible with the company's vision) away.

For example, Warren has clearly explained the ground rules based on which Berkshire Hathaway will be run. Now, when someone wants to invest there, they can look at these ground rules to decide whether they will be happy there or not. A few people may read these rules and decide not to invest, which is fine. No Hard Feelings. They will be happy elsewhere and Berkshire Hathaway will get other compatible partners (shareholders). This is good for everyone.

When we want to start or join a partnership of any size, any kind, we need to set or look for these ground rules. They are the real guidelines that help us decide whether a partner relationship is going to work or not. Those guidelines can be changed rarely with the full consent of all partners, but, once they are defined and published, everyone should respect them and follow them so that the environment is smooth and conducive to progress.

☑ **The Warren Lesson:** ***When looking for partners, find compatible ones, using a set of ground rules and expectations; keep all others out.***

75

Environment Makes Us

Today's newspaper has a story about a 14-year-old boy creating a mobile app to help war-torn countries and their citizens. This app connects people who want to donate money to such Nobel causes and people who actually need them.

This is a fantastic idea and the fact that a schoolboy has created it, gives us so much hope for the future. But, one interesting question remains: what made this boy build such an app when other students of his age are having fun or building fun things?

"Both my parents are software engineers who constantly discussed how technology can make a difference in people's lives", the boy says. "Similarly, my grandfather is a Gandhian who keeps talking about giving back to the society and serving others. As I grew up hearing their words, I started thinking in this direction."

With due respect to the boy's interest and efforts, he should be thankful that he was in the right place (house) and heard the right conversations which shaped his thoughts and actions. Many times, what we hear frequently has a deep impact on our thinking and guides us in the right (or wrong) direction.

"When I was a kid, I had the advantage of a home where people talked about interesting things", says Warren Buffett. He feels these conversations gave him new perspectives and made him visualise a world in which he wanted to live in and how he can contribute to the same.

Every child may not be as lucky as Warren or the boy who created the app described above to have parents who discuss interesting things. But, there are many other environments that can shape them in a good way. For example, school friends, teachers, college campus, societies he/she belongs to, office setting and so on. If we purposefully look for such intellectual environments and become part of them, we can learn a lot and get support and guidance for our early thoughts and activities. In addition, we can also contribute to others in the same environment as the support is mutual. This gives us the satisfaction of giving back to the society which helped us grow.

☑ **The Warren Lesson:** ***Seek environments where interesting conversations happen.***

76

Be Kind, Oh, Stranger

Life is full of surprises. They may come at a different pace at different times. But, no one can predict the exact path life is going to take. That's where it becomes important to plan for a situation where our plan doesn't go as per the plan.

For example, a common man can set aside a certain amount of money in a special account which takes care of 'x' months' expenses for his family. He won't touch this money under any circumstances. Even if he is forced to take it out, he will fill it as soon as possible so that this money always remains accessible for him and takes care of situations where he doesn't have an income for an extended time period.

Similarly, different people and companies set up different strategies to take care of unknowns that might happen. They may not be able to predict all the unknowns, but whatever they are able to think of, they will have a strategy to mitigate it.

However, Warren Buffett reminds us that when thinking of such strategies, we shouldn't be dependent on the kindness of strangers. If we do, then we are leaving too many things to others whom we don't even know. This results in a fake sense of security where we think the risk is taken care of, but in reality, it is not.

For example, if the common man in the example above keeps his "safety money" in the share market instead of his personal bank account, technically the money is still with him and it has the potential to grow in a better way year on year. But, if an unexpected event occurs and he needs to take out the money urgently, he is dependent on the strangers who are transacting on the share market to give him a kind price on that day. If they are not kind and the market moves down, he may not get the full amount and will suffer as a result.

Of course, this argument is not against investing in the share market. After all, we are learning from one of the greatest investors of all time and he would never say investing in shares is bad. However, in this particular example, the common man should've kept the money in his personal account instead of depending on the strangers' kindness. The main idea here is that depending on the kindness of strangers can backfire and give us a less than perfect situation. That's why Warren takes an approach of intentionally keeping his personal life and the companies he runs have a comfortable plan to withstand economic discontinuities on their own without depending on others, especially strangers.

☑ **The Warren Lesson:** ***Depending on the kindness of strangers is not a sound strategy; be independent, be on your own.***

77

The Cream-Skimming Approach

Dairies have a machine called a cream separator which draws off the cream from fresh milk. It does this easily by just picking the cream which is lighter and hence floats. This process is known as cream-skimming.

Warren Buffett recommends a similar approach when looking for companies to invest in or when finding managers to run those companies. He explains this process using the example of a basketball coach. When this coach is facing a crowd of students, he/she speaks to seven-footers, which are people above the average height. As height is one of the key factors in determining basketball success, one of those candidates the coach is speaking to is likely to be a suitable one for his/her team's needs.

Of course, there is no guarantee that someone taller will be a great basketball player. They may still need many other skills for them to be successful. But, when we think about the reverse scenario (someone having the skills, but not being tall enough to succeed), the benefits of this approach become clear.

Hence, if Warren wants to invest in a company and has a few options, he looks for seven-footers among them (those who satisfy his must have expectations). Once he finds one or two such options, he acts as a separator machine and does further research on those companies to decide whether to invest in them or not. All the other companies which didn't pass his seven-footer test are simply ignored. This gives Warren maximum time and energy to focus on deserving candidates. A similar approach is used when he is looking for the right people to fill roles in his companies.

There are arguments against the cream-skimming approach. Sometimes the criteria we use to skim may make us ignore a great candidate. In those cases, we should listen to the feedback and continuously improve the original criteria. Over time, we will become better at this which results in better shortlisting, focussed analysis of the shortlisted candidates and a faster, better decision.

☑ **The Warren Lesson:** ***When you have many options, follow the cream-skimming approach to pick a smaller set and focus on those options deeply.***

78

The Other Guy is Doing It

This may sound illogical. But, sometimes walking away from an opportunity is the most intelligent thing to do.

For example, a prospect is requesting quotes for a particular job and they have set the ground rules in terms of their expectations, budget, etc. Your organisation reads the requirements and arrives at a proposal that doesn't match these ground rules. You try to analyse it further to spot areas that can be improved so that you save costs and arrive at a workable budget. Even after this exercise, the proposal stands outside the limits set by the prospect.

In this case, you have two options: either talk to the prospect and explain to them that meeting all their needs with the given constraints is improbable, back up your argument with data and request for a change in the ground rules, or, walk away from the deal. There is no third option as you couldn't find a way to solve this problem with these constraints without losing money on your side.

While you are doing this analysis, you come to know that your competitor has already submitted a proposal to the same prospect agreeing to meet all demands within the given cost. What will you do?

Warren Buffett says that in this situation most companies will go ahead and submit a proposal from their side too even though they know it can't be done. They are doing this because they can't turn their back on business that is being accepted by their competitor. Hence, they decide to win this business to ensure the competitor doesn't get this.

But, if this game is played in the long run, it is our company that will be on the losing side. That's why Warren's advice is to walk away if the appropriate business can't be done. If the other guy is doing it, there is no condition that we should also do it.

Hence, when considering whether to pitch for an opportunity or not, our main and only decision criteria should be "can I meet these expectations in the given budget and still make the profit I desire?" If the answer is no, we shouldn't hesitate to walk away even if others are willing to do this business. Finding another suitable opportunity and spending our time there will be an intelligent investment of our resources.

☑ **The Warren Lesson:** ***If a business opportunity doesn't make sense to you, don't hesitate to walk away from it.***

79

Super Skill that Increases your Value by at Least 50%

Schools and colleges teach many lessons and skills to students. Depending on the stream chosen by those students they may not learn the same set of subjects, but some basic subjects are taught to almost all the students because they are essential for everyone.

Warren Buffett feels communication is one such skill that everyone should learn. He tells students that if they learn to communicate well in person (spoken communication) and in writing (for example, letters, e-mails, articles, proposals and other documents), they increase their value by at least 50%.

For example, if a student has a fantastic idea that he/she wants to research and get further help for implementing it, it is essential that the student speaks about it to a few people such as other students, teachers, potential sponsors, investors, government and private officials, etc, to convey what is in his/

her mind clearly. During these discussions, he/she may have to explain the original problem, pain points, proposed solution, expected benefits, returns (profit) and answer questions such as who is suffering, how many people are suffering, how is this solution different from other similar solutions, how it will be implemented, how much the implementation would cost, why it needs to be implemented now, why you are the right person to implement it etc. Sometimes he/she may only get a few minutes of time to explain all these and still make an impressive pitch and win the audience to their side.

The same example can be imagined as a written exercise as well. The student may be asked to submit a 4-page proposal explaining their idea and the quality of the document that determine how likely they are to get the required support.

While these examples focus on students, communication is an essential skill for everyone to succeed. Warren explains its importance by quoting a funny negative example: if you can't communicate well, it is like winking at a girl in the dark; not much will happen because of that.

☑ **The Warren Lesson:** ***Learn to communicate well.***

80

Finding Our Strength(s)

The history of the business world is ripe with examples of great people who changed the world, built big empires and made tons of money. New entrants to this world look up to them, get motivated and plan their journey with the hopes of reaching the top someday.

However, a careful analysis of these great people will give us two puzzling inputs: not all of them succeeded in their first business; not all of them succeeded with a unique solution that no one in the world has created before. If this is the case, what differentiates great business people from others who might fail or attempt something others have already done?

"The test is not whether you get the greatest business idea in the world for the first time", says Warren Buffett. "The test is whether you keep learning as you go to understand what your strengths are, what you can do to your customers, what you can bring to the party."

For example, let us say you are starting a restaurant in an area where a few other food options already exist. This by itself is not a bad idea just because others are also doing it. If you can differentiate yourself from others and focus on what you can do to win the customers' business, that can provide you with the winning edge. But, getting there is a continuous process where you may have to experiment with different options depending on your skills, market needs and other factors.

During this journey, great business people don't lose steam and they continue to wonder what their real strengths are. They continuously monitor the situation, listen to customers, understand their pain points, look at their personal resource set to see how they can solve them well and focus on their learning to fill the gaps if any. This entire process can extend beyond one business too. This means, their first or second entrepreneurial attempt may not be a great success as they didn't figure out their strength(s) then. Once they find their strength(s), their next attempt will be aligned to it and will bring them success.

☑ **The Warren Lesson:** ***Keep learning; Keep looking for your strengths.***

81

The Brain Work

The word "work" has evolved from humankind's early days to give different meanings in different centuries. For a caveman, work may mean actively going out and seeking food. A few centuries later, work meant preparing the land, growing food and collecting it. When the industrial revolution happened, work meant going to a factory and operating a machine. Around the same time, a white-collar work category emerged where people worked with pens, papers, files, typewriters and cabinets. Later the same people worked on their computers to achieve similar results.

While the meaning of the word "work" has changed a lot, it essentially means doing something with our hands. That's how humans earned their bread and got the comfort they needed. As this memory is very strong in our brains (and possibly in our genes too), we consider someone not doing anything with his/her hands as a lazy person. If someone sits in a corner and thinks about something, we ask him/her to get up and do some work.

In reality, someone can just sit alone and work too. They don't need to write down anything on a paper or a whiteboard and can simply think about various facts they collected by reading, listening to others, watching etc, connect the dots and make decisions for the future. This silent, invisible work can also bring good results in the right circumstances.

For example, if a company is continuously losing money on their production processes, an expert can observe the factory operations, its layout, various machines and workers and then think about possible improvements in these areas. Based on this, he/she can come up with a proposal that can help the company improve. This work happening in the expert's brain is as important as the work that happens in those hundreds of workers' hands.

'I insist on a lot of time being spent, almost every day, to just sit and think', says Warren Buffett. He understands that this is uncommon in American business as leaders are expected to 'get up and do something', not 'sit alone and think about what to do'. But, he doesn't believe in this general theory and spends a good amount of time every day reading and thinking. As a result, he believes he makes fewer impulse decisions than most people in business.

Moving continuously brings us progress. But, sometimes, the movement and the associated pressure can overwhelm us and cloud our thinking and decision-making process. This problem can only be resolved when we give ourselves time to stop and think. Today's knowledge workers and leaders need this time to digest all the information they are getting from various sources and to have clarity on the next steps. This investment will help them move beyond people who simply follow others' instructions and make them original thinkers who can come up with creative solutions to any problem.

☑ **The Warren Lesson:** ***Every day, spend some time sitting and thinking.***

82

The Narrow Vision

A company announces its forecasts every quarter. Later, they meet those numbers or exceed them or they may perform below their own forecasts.

This process looks harmless to an outsider: someone says they will hit some score; they are able to do it or not. That's it.

But, this seemingly simple process can introduce some serious issues in the organisation if those forecasts are considered as end games by themselves. That is, if everyone is only focusing on the forecasts of the current quarter and miss the big picture, it can result in some short term benefits, but in the long run, the company will suffer.

For example, let us say a company has announced $500 million as their quarterly forecast. But, when doing the actual calculations, they realise that they will be missing this forecast by $15 million. This company has met its forecasts for the past many quarters and they don't want to set a bad example by missing this. Hence, they find an R&D investment and move it to the next quarter. This adjusts the overall numbers, making them meet their original forecasts. This may be legally correct. But, the decision to postpone the R&D investment happened only because forecasts narrowed their focus to the current quarter, resulting in a possible long term loss by slow innovation.

"I tell my managers to pretend that this is the only business they and their family will own for the next 50 years and they can't sell it", says Warren Buffett. When leaders think from this perspective, missing a quarterly forecast doesn't look like a major issue and they will make the right decisions for the long term benefit of the organization.

Just like the quarterly forecasts for business leaders, we also may have short term goals and activities which cloud our vision and make us lose focus on the long-term goals and activities. We need to learn to spot them and adjust the perspective in the right manner to ensure we are not compromising long term success for some quick wins.

☑ **The Warren Lesson:** ***When making decisions, look at things from the long-term perspective, not from the short term perspective.***

83

An Unusual Race

You are participating in a race along with ten other people. The rules are simple: you all need to run a distance of 200 metres and the one who reaches the finish line first will be declared a winner.

So, all of you reach the starting line and get ready to run. The organiser says, "Ready on your mark, get, set, go."

When the organiser utters the word "Go", you suddenly find yourself 20 metres ahead of all other race participants. You don't know how; but, it has happened. For a moment don't worry about this being unfair to others. Just assume that you somehow got 20 metres ahead of all your competitors and it is not challenged by anyone. Will this give you a better chance of winning that race?

Of course, it would. As you are starting from 20 metres and all others are starting from 0 metres, you will only be covering a distance of 180 metres instead of 200 metres and you are likely to reach the finish line before others.

But, what if you are 20 metres behind all other competitors? What will it do to your winning chances?

It might affect you badly because you now need to cover a distance of 220 metres instead of 200 metres and all others would have an advantage over you. You may still win, but you need to put tremendous effort for that to happen.

Warren Buffett uses this beautiful example to explain how important it is for young people to be financially independent when they start their careers. When the career race starts, that is, when they come out of college, if they have some savings, skills, experience and network, they are equivalent to starting 20 metres ahead of all others. If they have a big debt to pay back and bad habits, it is the equivalent of starting 20 metres behind all others. Warren advises students to start thinking about it early and plan a better start to their active work life.

While this example suits perfectly for students, anyone of any age will find it to be true because being financially independent sets us free and gives us less anxiety about the future. Similarly, not being financially independent adds heavy pressure like swimming against the tide. When faced with such a situation, we should carefully analyse our commitments and see how we can make the race normal (instead of being behind others). Once this is achieved, the next step is finding ways to stay ahead of others so that we can definitely win.

☑ **The Warren Lesson:** ***Be financially independent, it sets you up for success.***

84

The Ideal Job

What is the ideal job for someone?

People accept a job for many reasons: money, power, fame, opportunity to do something good for the world, mental satisfaction of good work done, happiness in solving complex problems, helping others, leading others and so on. Each job may provide one or more of these benefits and people make the right selection based on their needs and expectations at that time. Hence, it is difficult to define 'the ideal job' and expect it to suit everyone in the world.

However, Warren Buffett suggests one general rule which fits in most scenarios for most people: look for a job that you would take if you don't need a job. Assume that you have everything you need and there is no need for you to work. At that time, what work will you take? That's the one that is likely to give you mental satisfaction even now.

For example, Warren does his work at Berkshire Hathaway not because it gives him a lot of money. The huge income he earns is only a byproduct and he does his work because he gets to work with fascinating people every day. That's his ideal job and something he would do (that is, he does) when he doesn't need a job.

Similarly, everyone has something which they absolutely love and would do it even if there are no other benefits. They may not get that opportunity in their very first job, or the second job, or the third job... but, Warren advises people not to give up and keep looking for it. When you find it, you know you have arrived.

However, when you are on this journey, those intermediate responsibilities and the benefits which come with them may try to deviate you from your search for your true love. That's when you need enormous control and understanding that the journey is still on and anything on the way is just a temporary arrangement. Only very few people find that ideal job and when they do, the satisfaction they get is priceless.

☑ **The Warren Lesson:** ***The ideal job for you is the job you would do if you don't need a job. Look for it and grab it when it appears.***

85

The Real Boss

The word "boss" is defined as "a person whose job is to give orders to others at work" in the dictionary. This person may be your manager or owner of the firm where you are working. These days they are usually not called "bosses", but there is no denying that he/she gets to boss you around.

When we look at the corporate hierarchy charts, another interesting fact emerges: most employees don't have a single boss. The boss has a boss, who in turn has another boss and depending on the level of an employee, he/she may have multiple bosses. Those higher level bosses may not talk to this employee on a regular basis, but they remain his/her bosses anyway.

However, there is one ultimate boss whom those employees can miss to notice amid all this hierarchical analysis: the customer. Irrespective of whether someone manages others or works in a desk or a machine, they all work for the customers' benefit and their paychecks are ultimately paid from the wallets of those customers.

For example, an employee may simply fix car parts in a factory and a supervisor can be his/her boss. But, both of them work for the customer who will drive that car someday and should always remember that in their mind, have fun and enjoy working for that customer. That's when true great work gets done because our best comes out when we keep our customers in the centre of our thinking and activities. With this, we understand the purpose of our work and it motivates us.

"Working for you [Berkshire Hathaway shareholders] turns our [Warren Buffett's and Charlie Munger's] jobs into fun and satisfaction", says Warren. "There is nothing more rewarding to Charlie and me than enjoying the trust of individual long-term shareholders who have joined us with the expectation that we would be the reliable custodian of their funds."

Similarly, customers of each one of us have placed their trust in us expecting us to take care of certain things well. Understanding them and addressing those needs gives ultimate happiness and satisfaction, making work meaningful.

☑ **The Warren Lesson:** ***Understand your true customers and take care of their needs.***

86

The 'No Games' Approach to Negotiation

Search for the word "negotiation techniques" in Google or Amazon. You will get hundreds, if not thousands of articles, videos, training courses and books promising to teach you many tricks for negotiating a better deal from anyone. They make you feel negotiation is a dirty art and those who don't know it will not be able to get the best value in their everyday transactions.

But, this common belief assumes that only one party (that is us) should win the negotiation and the other party should lose. The more they lose, the more we win because it is a zero-sum game. When you approach negotiation with this attitude, you need to learn many tricks so that you can squeeze every bit of value from the other party.

Warren Buffett, one of the most successful business negotiators of all time, says he doesn't do any tricks at a negotiation table. "I don't play games. I just say what I'll do and nothing else. People know, what I mean and what I am saying."

This means that when someone is negotiating with Warren, they hear the best deal early in the game, not later. Warren says what he can do clearly and doesn't keep his best cards for a future moment. This transparency makes the discussion go smoothly instead of wasting time on back and forth discussions and both parties guessing what is in the other's mind.

Also, this technique respects the other party. There is a genuine interest that the other party should win too and there should be a fair value exchange. As Warren has got such a reputation, people from all over the globe reach out to him when they want to sell their businesses. They know he will have the best interest of both parties in mind. Warren respects that and responds with a quote that he feels is workable. After that, some minor discussions can happen, but Warren's offer is already on the table, not hidden somewhere else to trick the other party.

Being transparent during negotiations may look dangerous. But, in a world where everyone seems to play games, there is huge value for being open-minded. If you make it clear and explicit, the other party will respect that and meet you on level ground.

☑ **The Warren Lesson:** ***Don't play games during negotiation; say what is there in your mind openly and take it forward from there.***

87

Cross-learning

Is Warren Buffett a great investor or a great businessperson?

Warren started his career as an investor. He helped himself and others by picking the right stocks to invest in so that their wealth can be grown. Later he started doing the same under his company where he invested in some businesses as a whole (outright purchases) or part (common stock purchases). As his company now owns many companies in multiple domains and actively looks for other such investments, he is considered a great businessperson too.

The interesting aspect is that Warren doesn't see them as two distinct things. While his thought process as an investor or as a business leader might be slightly different, he feels he applies learnings from one to the other. "My experience in business helps me as an investor and my investment experience has made me a better businessman", he says, "Each pursuit teaches lessons that are applicable to the other."

For example, a college professor writes a book in his field. His/her experience as an author gives him/her various skills such as researching, articulating thoughts and editing/rewriting them. These skills may be used by him/her while preparing for the next class or when teaching students. Similarly, he/she may use his experience as a professor when approaching the next book project.

Hence, lessons from a particular field or pursuit are not limited to that environment alone. In fact, cross-learning and applying thoughts from elsewhere refreshes us and does wonders by opening our minds to new possibilities.

But, what if we don't have another pursuit? What if we only have one role in one domain?

Even in that case, we play other personal roles such as husband/wife, father/mother, son/daughter, volunteer etc. which provides a wide range of experiences that can be used for our business pursuit. Similarly, we can apply what we learn as businesspeople in our personal roles. Idea is to keep our minds open and not apply learnings narrowly. If we move away from the thought that only boardroom thinking can solve business problems, suddenly the world will be full of interesting learnings that we can use.

☑ **The Warren Lesson:** ***Use lessons from one pursuit in another.***

88

Good Information and Quick Information

Do you have a reading feed?

We all do. They are the list of newspapers we read every day, television channels we watch, websites we browse, notifications we pay attention to and so on. These things combine and create a feed that we refer to very often and it acts as our information pool. This is where we observe the world and understand it better.

Technology has made news and information travel faster. Earlier, something happening in one corner of the world used to reach the other corner after a few days, sometimes after a few weeks, sometimes never. But now, everyone gets to know about everything immediately. As a result, we get information at such a pace that it becomes very difficult for us to digest and understand everything. Many times we feel like drinking from the fire hose.

However, Warren Buffett says his primary information source hasn't changed in the previous 40 years: annual reports.

This is surprising. When so much information about each and every company is coming into our reading feeds every day, every hour, how can we ignore all that and wait for the annual reports to come many months later?

Warren reminds us that judging a company needs good information, not quick information. Hence, he is okay to wait for a few weeks or a few months before the good information becomes available, ignoring anything which is quick and dirty.

This attitude can be applied to information about companies, countries, people and everything else. We don't have to feel anxious just because some quick information is continuously available. Instead of trying to chase all the breaking news, waiting for the good information to arrive is a better strategy as we would avoid the natural inaccuracies, ups and downs of such quick news items and can focus on the long term information which matters.

☑ **The Warren Lesson:** ***Good information is needed, not quick information.***

89

When your Hypothesis is Wrong...

You have a wonderful hypothesis that has the potential to become something big for yourself and your organisation. You discuss this with your boss and she is thrilled too. "Go ahead and get to the next level of details, write a proposal, we will make it happen", she says and gives you her full support.

For the next few weeks, you ignore other unimportant tasks so that you can focus on this matter entirely. You read books, speak to people and do experiments to get more details.

However, when doing this due diligence, you come to know that your original hypothesis may not be true. You understand its loopholes and weaknesses and suddenly it doesn't look like a great idea anymore.

In this situation, what will you do? Will you go to your boss and say, "Sorry, my original hypothesis is wrong. We better discontinue this line of thinking." Or will you continue your research hoping to get more material that can prove you right?

Warren Buffett uses the example of journalism to explain this and says many journalists would usually go for the second option. He calls it their 'greatest sin' because in this situation the best thing to do will be to give up that wrong hypothesis instead of going in the opposite direction trying to find proof for it. As a result, "there is a lot of momentum towards a lousy story. [Instead] you have to be able to say, "My hypothesis is no longer correct'. It is hard to do."

We all face such conflicts in our life even though we are not journalists. We continue to spend more time on a project just because we assumed something to be true and invested a lot of time in it. Instead of exiting that wrong thought process, we struggle to find evidence for our original assumptions. This leads to dual loss by creating anxiety in our minds (about not being able to prove our hypothesis and about being criticised by others) and by denying the opportunity for us to work on something else more meaningful. We need to swallow our pride and accept our mistakes so that we can move on to the next hypothesis. There is no shame in being wrong, as long as you accept it the moment you realise it.

☑ **The Warren Lesson:** ***Don't work on a wrong hypothesis just because you once thought it to be right. Declare it as wrong and move on to the next one.***

90

Looking for 1-foot Bars

A banker was passionate about dancing. She wanted to have her own dance school, perform on stages across the globe, appear on television and so on.

However, all these looked like distant dreams because at that time she only had skills and passion. No one knew her outside her small circle of friends. Hence, getting students or program opportunities was not easy. As a result, she was focusing on her banking job and kept postponing the steps that are necessary to make her dream a reality.

Warren Buffett has a piece of simple, practical advice to people like this banker-dancer, "I don't try to jump over 7-foot bars. I look around for 1-foot bars that I can step over."

If you are new to the art of jumping, it will be near impossible for you to jump over a 7-foot bar on the very first day. Hence, you would look for 1-foot bars that anybody can step over. Then, you will use that success and build on top of it. You will move slowly, but steadily and will conquer that 7-foot bar too.

For example, this banker-dancer can easily start her dance school with one student who could be a friend's child or a relative. Or, she can start a dance YouTube channel and showcase her talents to the world. These are 1-foot bars that she can manage even with her current newbie state. Once these are achieved, she will have the confidence to use them as a stepping stone and move to bigger and better things.

When we look at an enormous task, it looks impossible because the gap between where we are today and where we should be, is huge. However, we can identify and conquer smaller intermediate steps (1-foot bars and 2-foot bars) that can help us get there. These early wins will immediately give us confidence. They may look insignificant when compared to the ultimate goal that we want to achieve. But, they provide important motivation (for us) and social proof (for others) which prepare us mentally and physically for the next steps. Every success story across the world will have this pattern even though it is not visible to everyone.

☑ **The Warren Lesson:** ***Want to jump over a 7-foot bar someday? Start with 1-foot bars that you can easily jump over today.***

91

Loving What We Do

There is a small snack shop near our home where they sell a famous Indian delicacy called "Pani Puri". The young person who manages (and probably owns) that shop always has a smile in his eyes, handles any number of customers without issues and delivers tasty food fast. Even when the crowd is too much, his smile is intact and everyone can see that he enjoys what he is doing and not just doing it for the money.

One day I asked the gentleman how he learnt these skills. He explained that he got this interest during his college days, decided to intern with an expert and learnt it by practice. "I made many mistakes and the food I made was horrible. But, it was a good start and I improved from there. The main reason for my success was that I loved doing this."

Warren Buffett agrees with this young person when he says, "If you love something, you will get really good at it." As a teenager, Warren started loving investing/capital allocation and taught himself, learnt from others and improved, reaching the pinnacle of success. All these were possible because he loved it. When such love for a task or skill exists, you will find ways to become better at it because you enjoy the process.

For example, there are many executives who are experts in what they do. But, if we carefully notice, two patterns will be observable: they got better at it because of the love they had for the job and they didn't stop after becoming really good at it. They continue to invest time and learn new things because it is fun and enjoyable.

Hence, anyone who wants to become better at something should first find ways to love it. If you don't love teaching and want to become a top-class teacher, it is not going to work. Either start loving teaching or find another work that you love. This is because loving what we do is an important and must-have ingredient for success.

☑ **The Warren Lesson:** ***Love what you do; you will get really good at it.***

92

The Power of Habits

Many years back, Warren Buffett was addressing more than a hundred students in a Columbia University investing class. One of the students asked, "What can I do now so that I can prepare for a career in investing?"

Warren thought for a moment and then pointed to a pile of documents (reports, publications, papers etc.) he had brought with him. "Read 500 pages like this every day. All of you can do it, but I guarantee that not many of you will do it."

Reading relevant material every day might look like an oversimplified technique. But, Warren believes that knowledge can only be built up like that, like compound interest. As we read more, we know more, we understand better, we are able to connect the dots between various things we read/understood/ thought about at various times and the structure grows massively over many years.

As Warren explains, this can be done by anyone, but only a few will do it. This is because simple techniques look incapable of creating magic. But, even a great masterpiece is nothing but a collection of strokes. Each stroke created by the artist may look like simple lines, but the combined effect produces something wonderful. Similarly, daily habits such as reading or writing code or drawing or exercising or listening to experts add up and build our knowledge and skills. Practice makes us perfect and working on something every day gives us enough of that practice.

One of the common tools used by people to form a habit is marking a certain time in the calendar for the same. Warren reserves time every day for his reading and thinking. Similarly, we can also reserve time, even if it is 30 minutes per day, and dutifully start the habit we want to form. Recording the everyday progress and doing a weekly/monthly analysis also helps in moving in the right direction. But a bigger and better motivation will come when you see the compound effect which comes after a certain period. Till that magic happens, we can depend on the systems to keep us motivated. After we experience the magic, we wouldn't need any external reminders.

☑ **The Warren Lesson:** ***Find out what helps you win in your field, start doing it every day.***

93

Finding a Good Partner

Relationships are two-way streets. Both partners may not contribute in the same way, with the same role, but they both bring something to the table and benefit from each other. This is an implicit expectation whether it is a business relationship or personal.

For companies, finding the right partner can be a big enabler and something which helps them scale up, enter new territories, business lines, etc. However, finding the right partner is not easy and the cost of a wrong partnership is very high. Hence, companies tend to do long due diligence before signing the dotted line. They speak to potential organisations to understand their skills, experience and connections and ensure that their culture will be a good match too. Even after such elaborate filtering, some partnerships don't work and the companies part as friends (or foes) after a few failed attempts at working together.

Warren Buffett gives a simple solution to this problem, 'if you want to get a good partner, the way to do it is to be a good partner.' In other words, when looking for a potential partner, instead of focusing entirely on what the other person can bring to the table, also look at what you can do to them. How can you make them feel welcome in this relationship? How can you help them succeed? How can you enhance their strengths and help them address their weaknesses? How can you give them the best relationship experience? When focusing on questions like this, the default assumption that "I am perfect and I want nothing but a perfect partner" gives way to "I am looking for someone to grow with."

The same mindset is useful even after the partner is selected. When two companies or teams are working together, instead of one party playing the commanding role and always looking at the other party to follow instructions, both of them can try to be a good partner by collaborating together, co-creating solutions and building on each others' thoughts. When such a relationship is established where both partners respect each other and genuinely want to work together, even average companies can combine and create a masterpiece partnership. If this doesn't exist, even great companies can fail to work together.

☑ **The Warren Lesson:** ***If you need a good partner, be one.***

94

Only Twenty Punches

A few large beaches across the globe have a famous game called "Balloon Shooting" which people enjoy a lot. As the name suggests, there will be many inflated balloons fixed on a board and the players should try to shoot at them from a distance. Depending on the number of balloons they successfully hit, they might win a prize or just go back with fun memories.

One of the key rules of this game is that you are only given a certain number of bullets for each game. If you are not able to hit any balloon in those many attempts, you should accept defeat and give way to other players.

As people generally play this game for fun, they don't care much about this number of bullets rule or the possible defeat. They just try to shoot every bullet with as much precision as possible and that's it. Even if they don't hit any of the balloons, they wouldn't worry too much about it.

Imagine that a player playing this game is in desperate need of money. He has 6 bullets and can win a big jackpot if he hits 4 balloons. So, he takes a careful aim and shoots his first bullet.

Oops. Tough luck. It doesn't hit any of the balloons. His second bullet also gets the same result.

This means, this player has 4 bullets and has to hit 4 balloons with them. He can't make a mistake and every shooting has to result in a hit. In such a case, do you think he will be extra careful in his aiming and shooting when compared to all other players?

Of course, he would be. As he can't make any mistakes now, he will try everything possible to ensure success before pulling the trigger.

Warren Buffett recommends a similar attitude when taking investment decisions. He uses a punch card example which is similar to the balloon shooting game: assume that every time you make an investment pick, a single punch will be made in a punch card you carry. Once you reach 20 punches in that card, your investment game ends. You can't invest anymore anywhere.

In reality, such a card doesn't exist and no one can stop us from investing anywhere we want. But, Warren feels this freedom makes us not think enough before making a decision. It is like a balloon shooting game with an unlimited number of bullets. We will just randomly shoot and take the next bullet. Won't we?

Instead, if we assume that only 20 punches are allowed in the card, every investment decision we make will be well thought of. Even though such a restriction doesn't exist, having this mindset will help us avoid impulsive decisions and pick only the right stocks.

Even outside the investment world, deep analysis of available information before making a decision is recommended wherever feasible. Instead of assuming that we can do endless trials before hitting on the right solution, we can assume that the number of punches is restricted and we need to be thorough in our analysis.

☑ **The Warren Lesson:** ***Assume that you are allowed to make only a certain number of picks in life. That will make you analyse data thoroughly and carefully before every decision.***

95

The Light Calendar

Bill Gates, Founder of Microsoft and one of Warren Buffett's close friends, likes to fill every minute of his calendar with different tasks. He then goes ahead and finishes those tasks one after the other and feels good about it. According to him, that's the only way to work, that's the only way to do things.

One day, Warren showed his calendar to Bill. It was not empty, but there were only a few tasks here and there and compared to Bill's calendar, it was very light. When Bill expressed his surprise, Warren gave a simple answer, "A full calendar is not a proxy for your seriousness."

When you are good at something, it is natural that people around you, especially your coworkers, subordinates and partners, want your guidance. They want a slice of your calendar and you gladly create those slices day after day, week after week. Slowly, these requests from other people pile up and at some point, your calendar is controlled by them. You feel busy and important, but the reality is that you won't have enough slices left to do things that are important to you. This is why people with busy calendars are tired towards the end of the happy but rarely satisfied.

"You can't buy time", Warren declares. "Time is the only thing you can't buy. You better be careful about it."

Warren's way of keeping a light calendar is an indication of how careful he is about his own time. As he doesn't consider "filling the calendar with tasks" as the most important value addition from him, he is able to have a clear picture of what is important and which task deserves his time and how much time he should allocate to it. This is why he is able to spend more thinking time than many other contemporary business leaders.

With the introduction of digital calendars, we were supposed to have better control of our time and have a firm say in what we wanted to do at which time. But, ironically, they have become the primary reason for others to block our time which means we have very little left to us. There is no harm in helping others. But, we should first block our own calendar with the tasks which are essential and important for our immediate and long term commitments. The remaining time can be (carefully) shared with others to support their initiatives. This way we add value as individual contributors and as collaborators.

☑ **The Warren Lesson:** ***Be careful with your time.***

96

Intentional Confusion

You are reading the latest report from a company. But, even after a careful study, you are not able to understand it fully. Something feels wrong and the entire text is giving you confusion.

At this time, it is natural to imagine that we don't have the right skills to understand this text. After all, there are so many subjects in this world and one can't be an expert in all of them. Some information will go above our heads and we need to accept it.

While humility is an essential quality that everyone needs, Warren Buffett reminds us that in this case, our intelligence (or lack of it) may not be the real reason for the confusion. What if the author intentionally made it confusing?

But, why would someone do that?

When Warren reads accounting reports of a firm, he is looking for simple, clear facts presented in a way anyone can understand. This helps investors and the general public to get a good picture of what is happening in that company, where the money comes from, where it goes, how good is the organisation's financial health, etc.

However, some companies purposefully write these reports in a confusing way so that the answer to such important questions is ambiguous. This may be a trick they use to hide some bad news or internal wrongdoings. That's why even someone like Warren with decades of experience reading such reports gets confused when reading them.

Warren advises us to avoid a company if their accounting appears confusing because the confusion may be intentional and reveal the character of the management. If you are not in a position to avoid the company altogether, minimally you should ask the right questions and ask for better answers which clear the confusion.

There is another important angle to Warren's message. When we are writing something, we need to ensure that the reader gets clear answers to the typical questions with which they are coming to our text. If he/she gets confused when reading our text, our intention/integrity itself may come under the scanner. Hence, we need to be extremely careful to ensure all our communication is clear and transparent.

☑ **The Warren Lesson:** ***Clarity in communication is essential.***

97

Sitting on the Sidelines

One of my relatives is a regular investor in the stock market. Every month, he reserves a certain amount for his investments, researches a few companies of his interest, picks the right ones and spends his money on the right stocks.

My relative's employer pays him a performance bonus every six months. Depending on how well he performed during that half-year period, he gets a small, medium or large amount on top of his regular salary.

"Those are my toughest months", my relative says. "Having extra money is cool. But, when I have extra money, suddenly I want to spend it on stocks. I still do my research, but they are not as detailed as I normally do. As there is excess money in my account, I want to buy some stocks immediately and that pressure affects my judgement."

If this is the case with a small retail investor like my relative, imagine how companies with large piles of cash will be thinking about their investments. Will they make similar judgement errors and buy some shares at a very high price?

"Sit on the sidelines if you can't find investments of value based on your criteria", says Warren Buffett. "Many emotional investors make the mistake of buying at a very high price relative to value [just because they have excessive cash]."

When resources (such as cash) are in short supply or available in the exact amount required, using them effectively comes naturally to anyone because there are no other options. They need to think creatively to make the best use of the available resources and many great decisions are made due to this necessity. Bringing the same discipline when your resources are overflowing is tough. That's what differentiates normal people from experts. They don't act emotionally and look at the available resources as something that needs to be used as soon as possible. Every opportunity needs to be analysed based on the standard criteria that we use and the decision should only be dependent on this analysis. If no opportunity seems to pass those criteria, instead of throwing away the resources for the wrong cause, we should be patient and wait for the right opportunity to come.

☑ **The Warren Lesson:** ***Even if you have an abundance of resources, use them only on the right opportunities based on your criteria.***

98

Feeling Good About You!

How to extract the best from people?

This is a constant question faced by every manager, every boss and every entrepreneur. They have wonderful hiring processes; they analyse each profile carefully, picking the very best; they give them an amazing interview experience and ensure all skills are tested well before finalising the right candidate; they give the candidate an apt responsibility, a welcoming, yet challenging program, wonderful employee benefits along with constant encouragement. Yet, only a small percentage of those experts do well. Others either simply hang around or exit for better opportunities.

An organisation can grow only if it can rapidly get the right candidates in the right roles giving their best. This can't be random and we need a dependable, repeatable process that ensures this. Warren Buffett gives one such process: make them feel good about you.

Yes. Warren feels this is not about the other person's skills, experiences, or anything else. It is about your (the employer's) ability to make them feel good about you and your company. When they feel part of the organisation and like the people they work for, they naturally give their best because they want to. This intrinsic motivation is better than any extrinsic motivation the company can offer them.

When we review success stories of large companies with a specific focus on their early days, we find that many people joined those companies even before they became giants in their field. They may not have gotten a great salary or benefits, but they felt good about the company and decided to give their most productive years to it. As a result of many such contributions, the company grew and gave back to them. Later, the company has much better resources and is able to attract wonderful talent from the market. But, suddenly their ability to retain these talented individuals drops because of the same factor: are they feeling good about the company?

Making people feel good about us goes beyond the occasional praise or pat on the back. They should see meaning, passion in our work. They should find genuine care for them in us. They should see ability, interest from us to support them in their functions in whatever way we could. Instead of seeing them as yet another resource that any company needs to operate, their contribution should be respected and appreciated truly and openly. Actions should be consistent with words when decisions are made. When they know we always have their backs, they feel good about working for us as it is no more a simple business transaction. When everyone in a team feels this way, the effect becomes multifold and real great work gets done.

☑ **The Warren Lesson:** ***People will give their best if they feel good about you.***

99

The Confidence

Do you ever think about Oxygen?

Yes. Everyone knows that it is essential for our life and we all breathe in oxygen continuously. But, we think about all this only when someone asks a question. Otherwise, we take it for granted because it is always there and we get plenty of it.

However, if you are underwater for a few minutes or if the oxygen level goes down in your flight, suddenly you want oxygen. At that time, that's the only thing you think about and nothing else matters.

Warren Buffett uses this example to explain how important confidence is for a person's or a company's success. When they get plenty of it from everywhere, they don't even think about it. But, if they lose it for some reason, they immediately feel its absence and can't do anything else until it is restored.

For example, a famous chocolate brand enjoys the confidence of millions of customers as they buy it in large numbers every day. They use this as the vehicle for their growth and expand their company, enter new territories, introduce new product lines and so on. While doing all these, they don't realise that the confidence their customers have in their brand is the prime reason for their continued success because it is available in plenty.

Suddenly, a newspaper article declares that this brand's chocolate has a chemical that causes some serious health issues. The company denies this report with their test results and threatens to sue the newspaper. But, the public has lost confidence in the brand and that's when the company starts to notice it. Now their every step becomes slow and shaky because they have lost the business equivalent of oxygen and it would take time to get it back.

This applies to individuals too. When others keep their trust in us (due to our earlier accomplishments or other reasons), we don't take it seriously even though we enjoy and make the best use of that trust. If that trust breaks because of some reason, we immediately become aware of its absence and want it back. This happens because we don't realise its importance when it is available in abundance. Only after it goes away, we realise how essential it is for our survival. Pretty late response!

A better way of handling this will be recognising such oxygen-like aspects that we normally take for granted and making sure that we don't lose them carelessly. This ensures that our Oxygen supply is uninterrupted and we can enjoy a higher quality of life.

☑ **The Warren Lesson:** ***Confidence is like oxygen; when you have it, you don't think about it; when you lose it, that's the only thing you think about.***

100 Important Things

There is a gun with 100 chambers in it. One of those chambers has a bullet and all others are empty. This means that if someone places the gun on their own head and pulls the trigger, there is a 99% chance that they will survive. Very high odds. But, will anybody do that?

What if there is a one million dollar reward for doing this? Will this make some people try their luck? What about five million? Twenty million? One billion? We can keep on increasing the prize money, but an intelligent person won't play this game even though his/her chance of losing is only 1%. This is because that 1% worst-case scenario doesn't balance out the 99% best-case scenario. It is not a game worth playing.

"Don't risk something that is important to you for something that is not important to you, whatever be the odds", says Warren Buffett. In this case, if someone values their life and considers it more important than money, they won't play this game irrespective of the prize value or odds of success.

However, such situations in life are not as explicit as facing a gun with 99 empty chambers and 1 bullet. Hence, people might risk something that is important to them for something that is not important to them just because the odds seem to be in their favour. For example, rash driving mostly helps a person reach his/her destination faster; but, there is a chance of failure and the loss is much bigger when compared to the gain from the success. Here he/she is risking something that is important to them (their life) for something that is not important to them (saving a few minutes of driving time or the thrill of driving fast or winning a bet) and doesn't even realise it.

This is not an argument against risk-taking itself. Life will have some risks at any given point in time and we all should learn to analyse them, understand their probability, severity, possible impact, mitigations to avoid them, strategies to handle the worst-case scenario etc. and take calculated risks to progress. But, there are some risks that one should never take and some things one should never give away: doing things we love, with the people we love, helping others, keeping ourselves fit, spending time with our loved ones, giving back to society and enjoying life. When we realise these as must-haves and use them as the general rule in every decision-making, we will live a happy and contented life.

☑ **The Warren Lesson:** ***Don't risk things that are important to you, irrespective of the odds.***